Institutionalisation (and De-Institutionalisation) of Right-Wing Protest Parties

Institutionalisation (and De-Institutionalisation) of Right-Wing Protest Parties

The Progress Parties in Denmark and Norway

Robert Harmel, Lars G. Svåsand and
Hilmar Mjelde

ecpr PRESS

ROWMAN &
LITTLEFIELD
——— INTERNATIONAL

London • New York

Published by Rowman & Littlefield International, Ltd.
6 Tinworth Street, London SE11 5AL, United Kingdom
www.rowmaninternational.com

In partnership with the European Consortium for Political Research, Harbour House, 6-8 Hythe Quay, Colchester, CO2 8JF, United Kingdom

Rowman & Littlefield International Ltd.is an affiliate of Rowman & Littlefield
4501 Forbes Boulevard, Suite 200, Lanham, Maryland 20706, USA
With additional offices in Boulder, New York, Toronto (Canada), and Plymouth (UK)
www.rowman.com

British Library Cataloguing in Publication Data
A catalogue record for this book is available from the British Library

ISBN: HB 978-1-78660-739-3
      PB 978-1-78661-313-4

Library of Congress Cataloging-in-Publication Data Available

ISBN 978-1-78660-739-3 (cloth)
ISBN 978-1-78661-313-4 (paperback)
ISBN 978-1-78660-740-9 (electronic)

This book is dedicated to Clara Harmel, Arvid and Marion Mjelde, and to the memory of Clarence Harmel and Lars and Hedvig Svåsand. Without them, this book (and we) would not have been possible.

Contents

List of Abbreviations

AFL	Anti-Federalist League (United Kingdom)
CD	Centrum-demokraterne (Centre Democrats) (Denmark)
DNA	Det norske arbeiderparti (Labour Party) (Norway)
FI	Forza Italia (Italy)
FrP	Fremskridtspartiet (Progress Party) (Denmark)
FrP	Fremskrittspartiet (Progress Party) (Norway)
H	Høyre (Conservative Party) (Norway)
IdV	Italia dei Valori (Italy of Values) (Italy)
KF	Det Konservative Folkeparti (Conservative People's Party) (Denmark)
KrF	Kristelig Folkeparti (Christian People's Party) (Denmark and Norway)
LPF	List Pim Fortuyn (The Netherlands)
LT	Lega dei Ticinesi (Switzerland)
M5S	Movimento 5 Stelle (Five Star Movement) (Italy)
MP	Member of parliament
NATO	North Atlantic Treaty Organization
NSD	Norsk Samfunnsvitenskapelig Datatjeneste (Norwegian Social Science Data Services)
PD	Partito Democratico (Democratic Party) (Italy)
PdL	Il Popolo della Libertà (People of Freedom) (Italy)
PVV	Partij voor de Vrijheid (Party of Freedom) (The Netherlands)
RV	Radikale Venstre (Radical (Social) Liberal Party)
SD	Socialdemokraterne (Social Democratic Party) (Denmark)
SF	Socialistisk Folkeparti (Socialist People's Party) (Denmark)
SF	Sosialistisk Folkeparti (Socialist People's Party) (Norway)
Sp	Senterpartiet (Centre Party) (Norway)

SV   Sosialistisk Venstreparti (Socialist Left Party) (Norway)
UALS   Groupe d'union et d'action liberale et socials (France)
UDCA   Union de defense des commercants et des artisans (France)
UFF   Union et fraternite Francaise (France)
UKIP   United Kingdom Independence Party
V   Venstre (Liberal Party) (Denmark and Norway)
VG   *Verdens Gang* (Norwegian newspaper)
V,K,Z   Party initials for the Danish Liberal Party (V), Conservative
            Party (K), and Progress Party (Z)

List of Illustrations

Note: Captions provided with the figures are generally derivative from translations of captions that originally accompanied the figures. In some cases, additional information (e.g. date, location, or context) has been added from other sources.

List of Tables

Preface

Since the 1970s, hundreds of new political parties have been added to the established party systems of western European and Anglo-American democracies. Many of those parties have since fallen by the wayside, but others have gone on to reach institutionhood. And of course, some of the latter 'success stories' have then met with decay and de-institutionalisation. Among these developments, many have had marked consequences for the functioning and long-term stability of the party systems. Little wonder then, especially considering the simultaneous development (and success and failure) of many new parties in eastern and central Europe, that *institutionalisation* and its partner, *de-institutionalisation,* have become timely topics for party research! With this book, we hope to contribute to understanding of both of those topics.

Here we focus in particular upon the experiences of two similar parties, both of which were formed in the early 1970s, in similar countries with similar political systems. Both parties were of the *entrepreneurial right-wing protest* type which, according to theory and widely held expectations, were very unlikely to be more than a 'flash in the pan'. And yet both organised, succeeded, and survived to the extent that they could be considered fully institutionalised by the early 1990s. A major part of this book is devoted to explaining how that could have been possible for these two parties in particular, given the strong theoretical and practical reasons for expecting otherwise.

Though these two parties followed largely similar courses to institutionhood, their paths then diverged sharply, with one de-institutionalising and effectively failing, while the other continued to succeed and flourish. And hence the purpose for the second main part of the book: to explain these divergent paths for parties that started out so similarly.

Our main objective, of course, is to offer conceptual and theoretical frameworks that are more broadly applicable than just to the two parties that serve as our primary cases. Though the ultimate test of their generalisability must await additional systematic, comparative analyses which we hope will find inspiration from these pages, we do offer a few less-than-systematic generalisations in the final chapter of the book. In the appendix, we also provide some glimpses into experiences of other parties which share some of the distinguishing features of our two cases.

The primary theoretical takeaway from this book is that when it comes to party institutionalisation – at least for entrepreneurial right-wing protest parties – **leadership matters**! Or, to be more precise, parties of this type have specific leadership needs which must be met during each successive stage of the institutionalisation process – and then in post-institutionhood as well. Failure to match needs with skills can hamper progress toward institutionalisation of maturing parties, or even contribute to de-institutionalisation of parties that have actually reached institutionhood.

In the process of conducting our research, we have incurred many debts – too many to mention all of them, though we must highlight a few. On the top of that list must go the former leaders of the two Progress parties, Carl I. Hagen in Norway and Pia Kjærsgaard in Denmark, plus Peter Skaarup from the Danish People's Party. Each of them made themselves available for open-ended interviews with one or more authors of this book, early on in the process of gathering information. Their parties were also forthcoming with material whenever we requested it. Next on the list are the University of Bergen, Texas A&M University, and the University of Copenhagen; each of which was an excellent host to one or more of us as visiting scholars. The U.S., Norwegian, and Danish Fulbright Programs were instrumental in providing support for extended visits. The Norwegian Marshall Fund provided short-term assistance. Our friend and colleague Lars Bille, of the University of Copenhagen, was a source of useful information and advice throughout the early stages of the project. Finally, we thank Alexandra Segerberg and her colleagues at ECPR Press for their tremendous support at the end of the project. We are profoundly grateful to all of these organisations and individuals.

Part I

INTRODUCTION

Chapter 1

Introduction

Literally hundreds of new parties have been added to the party systems of well-established democracies since the 1960s. Most of those were a 'flash in the pan', so to speak, and died quickly, with little fanfare and little impact. But a smaller number survived, some of which gained what we call in these pages 'full institutionhood', not just enduring for a significant period of time, but also developing routinized procedures for carrying on party business and becoming 'forces to be reckoned with' (or at least acknowledged) by other parties in their systems. Among those, it has become almost a truism that most would be found on the left or in the centre of their countries' political spectrums, with 'right-wing protest parties' finding it particularly difficult, if not impossible, to institutionalise. And yet there have been *some*, and among those have been the Progress Party of Denmark and the Progress Party of Norway. Both were born in the early 1970s as additions to well-established party systems (and hence why we still call them 'new' parties), and both had fully institutionalised – by standards we develop in chapter 3 of this book – by the early 1990s.

While this book documents important facts about the development and experiences of those two parties, its primary purpose is to develop and demonstrate the utility of conceptual frameworks and theoretical approaches for the study of institutionalisation (and de-institutionalisation) of right-wing protest parties more generally, though much of what we do and find here has implications for the study of party institutionalisation (and de-institutionalisation) writ large. In the study of political parties, after all, as in any scientific endeavour, the main benefit from the study of 'deviant cases' is not the fun to be found in observing the deviates (though that can be fun), but instead the new theoretical insights which are required for understanding those cases and which have payoffs for explaining and predicting other cases as well.

For reasons we detail in chapter 5, the new right-wing protest parties of Denmark and Norway were not expected – by casual political observers but also serious party scholars in the political science community – to be more than a flash in the pan, and yet they defied the supposed odds against them and institutionalised within three decades of their births. How could that have happened? Were there particular circumstances or features of these parties and/or their environments which made it possible? If so, are those circumstances or features unique to these parties and their systems, or are they generalizable elsewhere? These are the questions which drive our inquiry in the first five chapters of this book.

In chapter 8, we turn our attention to the topic of organisational 'decay', or as we call it in these pages, 'de-institutionalisation'. Though both Progress parties were fully institutionalised by the early 1990s, only one of them survives today. Indeed, during the period from the mid-1990s through 2001, the Danish party went from institutionhood to demise. Since this happened for just one of the two parties and not both, we are presented with another puzzle: what factor(s) might help explain the de-institutionalisation of one institutionalised party while another avoids or effectively endures through episodes of decay, when the two parties share so much in common? Such is the 'stuff' of chapter 8.

Along the way, we have often found it useful to bridge existing literatures and theories as a means of spawning new insights and hypotheses. Partially as a result of this bridge-building, we have identified what we think are key factors in the stories of the Progress parties, which also help explain the special difficulties in the institutionalisation of parties like them and to explain the different trajectories of our two parties since achieving institutionhood.

At times, our attempts to learn from extant literature, and especially to cumulate from different literatures, were thwarted by conceptual fuzziness: the same term being used to mean different things, different terms being used to cover the same meaning, multidimensional concepts being treated as unidimensional, etc. And hence, we have tried in these pages to contribute to greater conceptual clarity regarding such terms as 'institutionalisation' and 'impact', not to mention 'right-wing protest party'. We turn now to a brief introduction to a few of the most important terms and concepts used throughout the book.

INTRODUCTION TO TERMS AND CONCEPTS

The term 'right-wing' party can be and has been applied to a wide variety of parties. In this book, we consider the Progress parties to be *right-wing protest parties of entrepreneurial origins*, and furthermore, though they were technically 'new' only in their earliest years, we and others still tend to refer to them as *new parties*. First, the Progress parties were from the outset *right-wing* in that they sought reduction in governmental intervention in the economy. For us, that condition is both necessary and sufficient to be classified as right-wing. Though others may associate, and indeed have done so, such stances as conservatism, authoritarianism, nationalism, and traditionalism with 'right-wing', we prefer to treat such additional traits as extra baggage which may accompany 'right-wingism', but which do not necessarily do so (as made clear in chapter 5). While their early stances on economic issues clearly placed both parties in the category of 'classically right-wing parties', it was substantially later (i.e. in the mid-1980s) that they added 'anti-immigration' to their issue profiles. For that reason, some consider the Progress parties to have become 'new-right' parties as well.[1]

Second, the Progress parties are *protest* parties, at least in origin, because the parties were chiefly identified with, and purposely emphasised, what they were *against* (i.e. taxes in particular), while leaving what they might be *for* as more of a mystery.[2] In overtly opposing establishment parties, some features of the establishment political process, and long-established policies associated with the political establishment, these two parties clearly qualified as *anti-establishment* parties as well.

Third, as parties of *entrepreneurial* origin the Progress parties are distinguished from parties that grew out of fully organised mass movements, but also from parties of parliamentary origin. Other 'personal' parties[3] have been formed by public office holders, but as entrepreneurial parties, each Progress party was the creation of one person who neither held an elected public office nor led a popular movement. Parties of entrepreneurial origin have most or all of the characteristics usually associated with 'charismatic' parties (e.g. see Panebianco 1988).[4]

Finally, we often in these pages refer to the Progress parties as 'new parties'. Though they were *literally* new at the time of their origins in the early 1970s, our meaning has more to do with their being additions to well-established party systems. In that sense, their 'newness' extends beyond what could technically be considered the period of their organisational youth. This is a point that plays heavily in our analysis in chapter 5.

Because *institutionalisation* is the central concept of this book, we should also make clear how we will use this term (in anticipation of a more detailed treatment in chapter 3). 'Institutionalisation' has been used in the political science literature – and even in just the literature on political parties – to mean several different things. While some (e.g. Rose and Mackie 1988) have equated a party being institutionalised with being recognised as an institution by outsiders, others (e.g. Panebianco 1988) have emphasised certain organisational attributes to the exclusion of external perceptions. Our own approach merges elements of each, while at the same time maintaining a distinction between institutionalisation and other related concepts such as organisational autonomy, organisational complexity, and centralisation of power. We define institutionalisation as 'the process of acquiring the properties of a durable organization which is valued in its own right and gaining the perceptions of others that it is such'. For us, then, institutionalisation is a multidimensional concept, encompassing: (1) 'internal' routinisation and value infusion, (2) 'external' perception of the party as having the ability to last, and (3) 'objective' durability. It is possible to be 'high' on one of these dimensions while 'low' on one or both of the others.

Relatedly, for us the term *'de-institutionalisation'* resembles Huntington's concept of institutional 'decay'. As such, de-institutionalisation refers either to discrete instances or to whole processes of reversal from indicators of institutionalisation: as when a party abandons routinized procedures, resumes features of 'charismatic' parties, or behaves in ways which cause other political actors to doubt its leaders' ability to endure or to deliver on promises.

ORGANISATION OF THE BOOK

This book is divided into four main parts. Part I, Introduction, consists of this chapter and the next. In chapter 2, we will introduce both the cases and their national contexts. Though the Progress parties are similar in many regards, they also differ in important respects, such as the timing of their electoral successes and failures and of their first, very important leadership changes. Similarly, the Danish and Norwegian political and party systems have much in common (enough so, in fact, that this study can appropriately be thought of as following the 'most similar systems' approach), such as comprehensive welfare state arrangements, cultural homogeneity, proportional representation, and, until 1973, stable multi-party systems. But they also vary in ways that will prove important for analyses in later parts of the book, such as facing different kinds of political problems and the timing of critical changes of personnel. Specific contextual factors will also come into play later in the book; for example, differences in the two countries' provision of public subsidies for parties.

Part II, Institutionalisation, consists of five chapters. In chapter 3, the concept of institutionalisation is developed in detail, and each of its three component dimensions is matched with appropriate indicators. Then in chapter 4 the conceptual framework is applied to the two Progress parties so as to determine the extent to which, and the ways in which, each of the parties was institutionalised as of the early 1990s, an important benchmark in our analyses. Though both parties are found to have been highly, if not completely, institutionalised by that time, interesting differences are found in the trajectories that the parties followed from their inception to institutionalisation.

Having established that both parties had in fact institutionalised, we devote chapters 5 through 7 to analysis of that accomplishment in the context of many predictions that they would die young and unfulfilled, in hopes of answering the question: 'what went wrong in the prognostications?' In chapter 5, special treatment is given to features which, according to extant theory on right-wing protest parties, should have rendered the Progress parties all but impossible to institutionalise. We also identify what we see as some very important offsetting factors, with special emphasis (in chapters 6 [theory] and chapter 7 [application]) on the need for particular leadership skills during different phases of the institutionalisation process, and the importance of timely leadership changes in making the new skills available within both Progress parties. Having established in chapter 4 that these parties had indeed institutionalised by the early 1990s, it is our objective in chapters 5 through 7 to contribute to explaining *how* such parties could institutionalise.

According to the broader extant literature on the concept of institutionalisation, completion of that process need not necessarily imply organisational permanence. To the contrary, fully institutionalised systems can fall into decay, increasingly show signs of de-institutionalisation, and even collapse entirely. Part III consists of chapter 8, which focuses on the topic of *de*-institutionalisation as applied to the Progress parties, or more precisely, the de-institutionalisation of Denmark's Progress Party during the last half of the 1990s. Because the Norwegian party did not suffer the same fate, we look for explanation in the different circumstances of the institutionalisation process in both parties (including *what* was institutionalised), as well as in differences in their immediate post-institutionalisation experiences.

Finally, in the concluding part (chapter 9), we recount the major findings of the previous chapters in an effort to identify factors from the stories of these two parties which should be considered in further refinements of theory on institutionalisation and de-institutionalisation of right-wing protest parties. In the process, we also provide some comparative context, drawing upon experiences of similar parties in other countries. The individual stories of several of those parties are told, in brief, in the appendix to the book.

TIME PERIODS FOR ANALYSES

The presentations in this book cover three time periods which roughly correspond in both countries to pre-Progress (pre-1973), the institutionalisation years (1973–1993/94), and post-institutionalisation (1993/94 and later).

Chapter 2 introduces not only the Progress parties, but also the contexts within which they developed, obviously including the pre-Progress years.

Throughout the empirical chapters of Part II (Institutionalisation), our analyses focus upon the period from the birth of the Progress parties in the early 1970s through the early 1990s. By the end of that time period, both parties had existed for approximately two decades and had, in various ways, become routinized and integrated within their respective party systems, and thus institutionalised. In 1994/95, both parties suffered serious splits. For the Norwegian party, this proved to be an important test of survivability, which the party passed, and indeed that party continues to this day. For the Danish party, though, the split proved to be a major component of the process of decay, significantly contributing to de-institutionalisation and eventually to the demise of the party. As will be detailed in chapter 8, that de-institutionalisation process covered the period from the mid-1990s through 2001, after which the party was never able again to garner sufficient support for recertification.

Thus, while material in the book spans the post–World War II era through recent years, the greatest concentration will be on developments from the early 1970s through early 2000s.

RESEARCH DESIGN(S)

In different places and for different purposes, we employ variants of both similar systems and different systems designs in this book. Because both of the Progress parties had completely institutionalised by the early 1990s, while others of the 'right-wing protest' and 'charismatic' parties have generally found it difficult to do so, we look especially for plausible explanation from features which our two Scandinavian parties (and/or their environments) have in common but which separate them from those other parties (and/or their environments).[5] But when seeking reasonable explanation for why the two parties institutionalised differently (i.e. why they institutionalised different patterns of behaviour) and why one eventually de-institutionalised while the other has not, we of course turn to other aspects on which the two parties (and/or their environments) also differ.[6]

NOTES

1. Others that are normally included in the category of new-right parties are, for instance, the Vlaams Belang in Belgium, the True Finns in Finland, the Sweden Democrats in Sweden, and the Republikaner in Germany.

2. The terms 'anti-establishment' or 'protest' party locate new parties in opposition to the existing policy areas dominating the political discourse. Such parties include the Centre Democrats in the Netherlands, the Front National in France, and the Lega Nord in Italy. For research on such parties, see the special issue of the *European Journal of Political Research* on 'The Politics of Anti-Party Sentiment', edited by Poguntke and Scarrow (1986). See also Ivarsflaten and Gudbrandsen 2013.

3. See Verseci 2015; Levitt and Kostadinova 2014.

4. However, not all entrepreneurial parties are charismatic in the same way. Though all are creations and creatures of their leaders (who may or may not have personal charisma), and hence all are charismatic parties (according to Panebianco's definition; see pp. 145–147), some emphasize 'issues' in the message the leader creates, while for others the leader (that is, the leader's supposed ability to do great things) *is* the party's message. The Progress parties and most other European entrepreneurial parties are of the former variety. Entrepreneurial 'person' parties are often found in developing democracies, where such parties are often developed to support the candidacy of just a single presidential candidate. Such parties are more likely to be associated with the notion of 'personal charisma' than is the case for entrepreneurial 'issue' parties such as the Progress parties. Unless otherwise noted, the arguments of this book are not intended to be generalized to entrepreneurial 'person' parties.

5. We should be clear that in this book our comparison of the two Progress parties to one another is explicit and systematic, while comparison to other cases is largely implicit and when made explicit, is generally less systematic and more illustrative and suggestive.

6. Or to state it differently – and in a way more valid to the underlying logic of the design – we do *not* seek explanation for similarities from the many things on which the cases differ, nor do we seek explanation for differences from the many things on which they are alike.

Chapter 2

The Cases and their Contexts

From World War II until 1973, the Danish and Norwegian party systems could be, and indeed often were, described as stable, almost sleepy, five-party systems. So stable were the patterns that they seemed to be prototypes for Lipset and Rokkan's (1967) 'frozen' party systems.

But in 1973, all ice broke loose (Pedersen 1987; Valen 1981). It involved not only shaken party allegiances, but also the development of several new parties in each country. In Denmark, the number of parties represented in the Folketing (the Danish parliament) increased from five to ten, and in Norway two new parties won seats (see Tables 2.1a and 2.1b). Among the new parties in both countries were right-wing parties that would prove to be among the more enduring and in many ways the most surprising and most significant of the newcomers. They are the focus of our case analyses in this book. Though we will provide much detail on these parties throughout the book, it is our purpose in this chapter to introduce them to readers who don't yet know them, and then to briefly describe the national contexts within which these parties arose and did so surprisingly well.

THE CASES: THE PROGRESS PARTIES
OF DENMARK AND NORWAY

In these pages, we will briefly tell the stories of the Progress parties, covering the period from party formation through institutionalisation – that is, the early 1970s through the mid-1990s – for both parties. In chapter 8, we will cover more recent years (through 2001, as the Danish party experienced de-institutionalisation) and beyond (as the Norwegian party continued to thrive).

Table 2.1a   Election Results (Number of Seats and Percentage of Votes)

									Denmark[1]									
	'68	'71	'73	'75	'77	'79	'81	'84	'87	'88	'90	'94	'98	'01	'05	'07	'11	'15
FrP	–	–	28	24	26	20	16	6	9	16	12	11	4	–	–	–	–	–
	–	–	15.9	13.6	14.6	11.0	8.9	3.6	4.8	8.9	6.4	6.4	2.4	0.6	–	–	–	–
DF	–	–	–	–	–	–	–	–	–	–	–	–	13	22	24	25	22	37
	–	–	–	–	–	–	–	–	–	–	–	–	7.4	12.0	13.3	13.9	12.3	21.1
KF	37	31	16	10	15	22	26	42	38	35	30	27	16	16	19	18	8	6
	20.4	16.3	9.2	5.5	8.5	12.5	14.5	23.4	20.8	19.3	16.0	15.0	8.9	9.1	10.3	10.4	4.9	3.4
V	37	30	22	42	21	22	20	22	19	22	29	42	42	56	52	46	47	34
	18.6	15.6	12.3	23.3	12.0	12.5	11.3	12.1	10.5	11.8	15.8	23.3	24	31.3	29.0	26.2	26.7	19.5
CD	–	–	14	4	11	6	15	8	9	9	9	5	8	–	–	–	–	–
	–	–	7.8	2.2	6.4	3.2	8.3	4.6	4.8	4.7	5.1	2.8	4.3	1.8	1.0	–	–	–
KrF	–	0	7	9	6	5	4	5	4	4	4	0	4	4	–	–	–	–
	–	2.0	4.0	5.3	3.4	2.6	2.3	2.7	2.4	2.0	2.3	1.8	2.5	2.3	1.7	0.9	0.8	–
RV	27	27	20	13	6	10	9	10	11	10	7	8	7	9	16	9	17	8
	15.0	14.4	11.2	7.1	3.6	5.4	5.1	5.5	6.2	5.6	3.5	4.6	3.9	5.2	9.2	5.1	9.5	4.6
SD	62	70	46	53	65	68	59	56	54	55	69	62	63	52	47	45	44	47
	34.2	37.3	25.6	29.9	37.0	38.3	32.9	31.6	29.3	29.8	37.4	34.6	36.0	29.1	25.8	25.5	24.9	26.3
SF	11	17	11	9	7	11	21	21	27	24	15	13	13	12	11	23	16	7
	6.1	9.1	6.0	5.0	3.9	5.9	11.3	11.5	14.6	12.9	8.3	7.3	7.5	6.4	6.0	13.0	9.2	4.2
EL	–	–	–	–	–	–	–	–	–	–	–	6	5	4	6	4	12	14
	–	–	–	–	–	–	–	–	–	–	1.7	3.1	2.7	2.4	3.4	2.2	6.7	7.8

LA	–	–	–	–	–	–	–	–	–	–	–	5 / 2.8	9 / 5.0	13 / 7.5
A	–	–	–	–	–	–	–	–	–	–	–	–	–	9 / 4.8

Total number of seats in the Folketing: 175
FrP = Progress Party (Fremskridtspartiet)
DF = Danish People's Party (Danske Folkeparti)
KF = Conservative People's Party (Det Konservative Folkeparti)
V = Liberal Party (Venstre)
CD = Centre Democrats (Centrum-Demokraterne)
KrF = Christian People's Party (Kristelig Folkeparti)
RV = Radical (Social) Liberal Party (Radikale Venstre)
SD = Social Democratic Party (Socialdemokratiet)
SF = Socialist People's Party (Socialistisk Folkeparti)
EL = Unity List (Left) Enhedslisten
LA = Liberal Alliance (Liberal Alliance)
A = The Alternative (Alternativet)

Source: http://www.parties-and-elections.eu/denmark2a.html
[1] In 1973, three brand-new parties – the Progress Party, the Centre Democrats, and the Christian People's Party – entered parliament. Two additional ones – the Justice Party and the Communists – re-entered parliament. By 1981, however, both were out of parliament again and have therefore been left out of table 2.1a.

Table 2.1b Election Results (Number of Seats and Percentage of Votes)

							Norway[1]						
	'65	'69	'73	'77	'81	'85	'89	'93	'97	'01	'05	'09	'13
FrP	–	–	4	0	4	2	22	10	25	25	38	41	29
	–	–	5.0	1.9	4.5	3.7	13.0	6.3	15.3	14.6	22.1	22.9	16.3
H	31	29	29	41	53	50	37	28	23	38	23	30	48
	21.1	19.6	17.4	24.8	31.7	30.4	22.2	17.4	14.3	21.2	14.1	17.2	26.8
V	18	13	2	2	2	0	0	1	6	2	10	2	9
	10.4	9.4	3.5	3.2	3.9	3.1	3.2	3.6	4.4	3.9	5.9	3.9	5.2
KrF	13	14	20	22	15	16	14	13	25	22	11	10	10
	8.1	9.4	12.2	12.4	9.4	8.3	8.5	7.9	13.7	12.4	6.8	5.5	5.6
SP	18	20	21	12	11	12	11	32	11	10	11	11	10
	9.9	10.5	11.0	8.6	6.7	6.6	6.5	16.8	8.0	5.6	6.5	6.2	5.5
DNA	68	74	62	76	66	71	63	67	65	43	61	64	55
	43.1	46.6	35.4	42.2	37.1	40.7	34.4	36.9	35.1	24.3	32.7	35.4	30.8
SV	2	0	16	2	4	6	17	13	9	23	15	11	7
	6.0	3.5	11.2	4.2	4.9	5.5	10.0	7.9	6.0	12.5	8.8	6.2	4.1

Total number of seats in Storting: 150 ('65–69); 155 ('73–81); 157 ('85); 165 ('89–01); 169 ('05–13)
FrP = Progress Party (Fremskrittspartiet)
H = Conservative Party (Høyre)
V = Liberal Party (Venstre)
KrF = Christian People's Party (Kristelig Folkeparti)
SP = Centre Party (Senterpartiet)
DNA = Labour Party (Arbeiderpartiet)
SV = Socialist Left Party (Sosialistisk Vesntreparti)
Source: http://www.parties-and-elections.eu/norway2.html
[1]In 1973, two brand-new parties – the Progress Party and the New People's Party entered parliament. The Socialist People's Party (SV) re-entered parliament. The New People's Party merged with the Liberals in 1988.

Figure 2.1   Mogens Glistrup in Copenhagen on 17 February 1978. *Credit*: EXPRESSEN; *Photographer*: Torbjörn Andersson/EXP/TT.

The Danish Party

In 1972 Danish tax lawyer Mogens Glistrup decided to form a new party for the purpose of focusing attention on his crusade against high taxes.[1] On 22 August of that year, at a small gathering at a restaurant in Tivoli Gardens amusement park, he announced his decision to the media and the public. He then set about to single-handedly develop a platform that would clearly distinguish his 'one man fight against the system' (his words) from the rest of Denmark's parties (Glistrup 1978: 2). The resulting document concentrated on just three main points: 'income tax, red tape bureaucracy, and the jungle of laws and regulations' (*Morgenposten*, 18 March 1973, quoted in Damborg and Østerby 1973: 50).

Though the party did not have roots in a well-established social movement, it did have roots in something of an ad hoc political movement that Glistrup himself had begun in 1971, and in which his personal abilities would replace the need for an organisation. In a television appearance early that year, on a weekend when most Danes were completing – or had just completed – their tax returns, Glistrup had stunned much of Denmark and apparently tantalised part of it with his carefully prepared anti-tax message. As he recalled later:

> I used the two minutes to tell the public that no one had to pay more income tax than he wanted, that the tax evaders were as heroic as the resistance groups

during World War II's German occupation, and that people suffering from tax diseases ought to consult a tax doctor as they would consult a dentist if they had a toothache. (Glistrup 1978: 2)

By the time Glistrup's Progress Party (Fremskridtspartiet) made its election debut in the 4 December 1973 elections, its leader had garnered enough attention for himself and his party that it would pull fully 15.9 per cent of the votes and win twenty-eight of the 179 seats in the Folketing,[2] making it the second-largest party in parliament and an overnight success. For two more elections, the party enjoyed almost the same performance, winning twenty-four seats (with 13.6 per cent of the vote) in 1975 and twenty-six seats (with 14.6 per cent of the vote) in 1977.

But then the party's electoral fortunes began to decline: first to twenty seats (11.0 per cent of the vote) in 1979, then sixteen seats (8.9 per cent of the vote) in 1981, and then just six seats (3.6 per cent of the vote) in 1984. Not coincidentally, Glistrup had lost his personal fight with the tax bureau in 1983,[3] and spent eighteen months (31 August 1983–11 March 1985) behind bars for tax evasion. The negative media attention surrounding the case undoubtedly affected Progress's electoral performance, but for some pundits, the declining fortunes were affirmation of early predictions that this would be just another 'flash in the pan' protest party. However, the self-congratulations were as premature as the predictions would prove to be wrong. Towards the end of the 1980s the party's electoral fortunes improved again. It's number of seats and vote share increased to nine seats and 4.8 per cent of the votes in 1987 and further to sixteen seats and 8.9 per cent of the vote in 1988. Although the 1990 and 1994 elections were less successful, with twelve and eleven seats respectively, the party was still large compared to several others in the Folketing.

During the period of Glistrup's physical absence from the party's headquarters, a new leadership emerged within the parliamentary wing. Although Glistrup had dominated the party from its start, he had for the most part done so without holding formal leadership positions.[4] His term in prison created opportunities for those in official positions to step forward as effective party leaders. A veteran of the party, Helge Dohrmann, had already become chair of the parliamentary group in September 1983. When Glistrup began his prison term, Dohrmann assumed more of the day-to-day responsibilities for running the party. But responsibility for speaking on the party's behalf would increasingly be shared with a parliamentary newcomer, Pia Kjærsgaard, who assumed Glistrup's seat when he departed for prison.[5] In October 1984 she was elected to the position of political spokesperson, from which she would effectively share leadership of the party with Dohrmann until his death in September 1989. As the party's effective leaders, Dohrmann and Kjærsgaard

Figure 2.2 **Mogens Glistrup, Pia Kjærsgaard, and Helge Dohrmann at a Progress Party meeting on 9 January 1984.** *Credit*: Scanpix Denmark; *Photographer*: Palle Hedeman.

differed from Glistrup in two important regards. Both were less personally charismatic (and certainly less flamboyant and notorious) than Glistrup, and both (but particularly Kjærsgaard) were more prone to making the party acceptable to the 'mainstream' of Danish politics. Though they found support for normalising the party, the job would not be an easy one.

Even during his time in prison, Glistrup's presence was clearly felt within the party. As Dohrmann and Kjærsgaard used their positions as parliamentary group leaders to develop a more 'normal' organisational style and campaign profile, Glistrup functioned, due to his role as founder and his position as a board member for life (guaranteed to him in the party's constitution), as the focal point for both media coverage outside and his own loyal followers inside the party. In spite of the predictable infighting, though, the party began its electoral comeback over the next few elections. Having served as the #1 public face for the party during those campaigns, Kjærsgaard would now be seen as its new saviour, and was clearly poised to solidify her position as its leader.

Though the sharing relationship with Dohrmann increasingly favoured Kjærsgaard after 1987, and ended abruptly upon Dohrmann's death in 1989, Glistrup's return to the Folketing group in 1987 marked the beginning of a period of heated conflict between the founder and the official spokesperson. Finally moving in 1990 to end what Kjærsgaard had come to see as her biggest organisational problem, the majority in the party engineered a policy of parliamentary discipline under which Glistrup would effectively be denied renomination that same year.[6] A year later, it would muster the two-thirds majority vote necessary to negate his claim to a position on the main board for life. The party that had begun as anti-organisational had by now developed a more normal organisational style. The party that had begun as the personal creation of Mogens Glistrup had endured his term in prison and his replacement in leadership.

In the 1990 election the party lost a few seats, but remained at a respectable 6.4 per cent of the vote, winning twelve seats in the Folketing. Kjærsgaard's strategy to make the party credible in the eyes of the other non-socialist parties would now culminate in the so-called 100-points programme for the 1994 election.[7] The aim was to provide a political basis for parliamentary cooperation between Progress, the Liberals, and the Conservatives, and the latter two parties reacted positively though stopped short of committing themselves. In the election of 1994 the three parties together failed to win sufficient seats to replace the coalition led by the Social Democrats. Progress itself lost one seat, and this perceived defeat reopened the old cleavage between Pia Kjærsgaard's pragmatists (nicknamed the *Pia*nists) and the party's hardliners. With Kjærsgaard's faction a minority in the parliamentary group, and with her candidates losing important leadership elections, she and three fellow MPs split and formed a new party in 1995 – the Danish People's Party. Though Progress, under different leadership, did continue parliamentary representation for several more years, it never truly recovered from that split.[8] Nevertheless, having survived for two decades organisationally and in parliament, the Progress Party had obviously been no flash in the pan.

The Norwegian Party

In 1973, sixty-nine-year-old dog kennel owner Anders Lange announced that he was ready to form his own version of Glistrup's party in Norway. He did so in an Oslo theatre, espousing the same anti-tax message as his kindred spirit in Denmark. Hardly a polished speaker, Lange nonetheless entertained his audience with stories of personal experiences that related to abuses of the welfare state and, not unrelatedly, misuses of the taxpayers' hard-earned 'kroners'. Whereas the established parties might differ among themselves on how to spend those kroners, the new party would be unique in questioning not only the level of taxation, but some of the basic aspects of the welfare state as well.

Like Glistrup's Progress Party, Lange's 'Anders Lange's Party for a Strong Reduction in Taxes, Rates, and Public Intervention' clearly had entrepreneurial beginnings in a self-built 'movement'. The groundwork for this movement had been laid several years before Glistrup held his first meeting in Tivoli Gardens. For approximately fifteen years prior to announcing formation of his new party, Lange had published a combination dog owners' magazine/ political newsletter in which he freely shared his right-wing views with subscribers. When he announced the meeting to organise the party, a crowd of approximately one thousand heard and answered the call. But while the enlistment may have started earlier in Norway than in Denmark, it was still very much 'Lange's army' that the volunteers were joining.

And like Glistrup, Lange emphasised the distinctiveness of his party from the others. This party was to be different from all the rest not only in its platform, which was already distinctive enough, but also in its form: something of an 'anti-party' party. Strongly preferring decision-making by 'spontaneous action' to normal party organisation, Lange firmly believed that a loose movement with strong leadership would result in more responsive decisions than a more highly organised and decentralised party of the traditional type. He had no desire to emulate what he sarcastically called the 'old-time parties'.

The Norwegian party did not duplicate Glistrup's electoral success in its first election, but did better than most new parties do (see Harmel and Robertson 1985 and Bolleyer 2013), winning 5.0 per cent of the vote and four seats in the Storting (Norway's parliament). Then a highly visible split from the party in 1974 and Lange's death a few months later dealt double blows to the new party. In 1977 it won just 1.9 per cent of the vote and no seats, giving credence to predictions of many observers – politicos and academics alike – that the Norwegian version of Glistrup's party would 'flash' and then disappear. But these predictions would prove to be as faulty as their Danish counterparts.

In the years following Lange's death, his party tried two other leaders, but neither could regenerate the original enthusiasm of Lange's supporters. Then,

Figure 2.3   At the National Congress of Anders Lange's Party on 28 January 1974. Carl I. Hagen (standing, second from right) and Kristoffer Almås share a toast with Anders Lange (far left). However, when the figure was first published, the newspaper caption noted 'but afterwards the turmoil continued'. *Credit*: VG; *Photographer*: VG.

in what might now be seen as a stroke of political brilliance, the party in 1978 selected a one-time follower and then nemesis of Lange, a young man by the name of Carl I. Hagen, to be its leader. Hagen had been in the audience at the founding meeting of the party, and within weeks had found himself in the informal position of party secretary.[9] But even at the age of twenty-nine, Hagen had his own vision of how parties should look and act, and his vision was substantially at odds with Lange's. After arguing, to no avail, that a party should differ from others in what it says but *not* in how it acts, Hagen parted company with Lange and a few months later joined the splinter Reform Party.[10] The splitting of anti-tax votes was certain to prove difficult for both parties to overcome. Less than a year after Lange's death, Hagen returned to his former party, which was then renamed 'Fremskrittspartiet' (the Progress Party).

In the year after the party's dramatic loss of all four seats in 1977, Progress elected Hagen as chair, and he moved quickly to accomplish his vision for the party: normalising its organisational structure and substantially broadening its program. In the next election, in 1981, the party won four seats with 4.5 per cent of the vote. A slight setback in 1985 – dropping to two seats with 3.7 per cent of the vote – was followed by a major success in 1989, jumping to twenty-two seats and 13.0 per cent of the vote. Though aided by mistakes made by other parties (see Strøm 1996), Hagen was justifiably credited with making the most of the opportunity presented to his fledgling party.

As important as that victory was for boosting morale within the party, circumstances surrounding a marked downturn four years later were equally important to contributing to internal strife and a revolt against Hagen's leadership. The 1993 election was totally dominated by the issue of Norwegian membership in the European Union. In a desperate attempt to regain the initiative in the face of marginalisation of his party's main concerns, Hagen had boldly announced – without prior consultations in his party – that Progress would not push for lower personal taxes in the next government. That action, which was seen as heretical by some in the party, combined with the electoral downturn – to just 6.3 per cent of the vote and ten seats – to trigger a revolt against Hagen's leadership among provincial leaders. In the aftermath of the election, the Progress's youth organisation dissolved itself, and eventually four members of the parliamentary group broke from the party.[11] But when all was said and done, the party – though battered and bruised – survived the ordeal and continued its dependency on the strong personality of Hagen as its leader.

That dependency, coupled with nagging problems of factionalism and resignations, had left some observers still questioning in the mid-1990s (the endpoint for our analyses of chapters 4 through 7) the permanence of what was often called 'Hagen's party'. But regardless what the future would bring, the Norwegian party had already joined its Danish counterpart in proving the pundits wrong. By their durability, their ability to adapt to environmental propensities regarding organisation, and their records of electoral performance, the two Progress parties had clearly demonstrated that they had not been simply a 'flash in the pan'.

THE CONTEXTS: THE DANISH AND NORWEGIAN POLITICAL SYSTEMS

To the non-Scandinavian, the Nordic countries have always seemed more similar to each other than different, and it is indeed the case that a range of economic, cultural, and political factors has distinguished the Scandinavian countries as a group from other European countries. Expressions such as 'the Scandinavian five party model' (Berglund and Lindstrøm 1978) and 'the Scandinavian welfare state model' (Kuhnle 1983) highlight such similarities.

The two Scandinavian countries of most interest to us here – Denmark and Norway – certainly share many political attributes. Although not adjoined physically, the two countries share an almost 400-year period of history when Norway was part of the Danish-Norwegian kingdom. And yet, in spite of basic similarities, there are important differences in detail.

For purposes of this book, it suffices to briefly describe the systems along six aspects of politico-economic orientation, governmental institutions, and political competition which are especially important for understanding the place of new parties – and particularly their level of success – in a political system: politico-economic orientation, parliamentary arrangements, the electoral system and rules for distributing seats, the party system, traditional patterns of government formation, and the nature of established party organisations. Though much of our discussion is cast in the present tense, it can be assumed that we are also describing the contexts as they were during our earlier periods of analysis, unless otherwise noted.

Politico-economic Orientation

A key feature of politics and government in both Denmark and Norway has been – at least since the late 1930s – the centrality of the tenets and institutions of what has come to be known as 'Scandinavian social democracy' (Arter 1999; Castles 1966; Einhorn and Logue 1989). Beyond the fact that Social Democratic parties have tended to be the most popular in these systems, there is a deeply engrained political orientation to which all of the major parties have generally subscribed (at least until advent of the Progress parties), including many of the goals of social democracy and a reliance on the public sector to implement those goals. Before coming to power in the mid-1960s, the non-socialist parties of Denmark and Norway had to a large extent incorporated into their programs an acceptance of the 'welfare state' including state responsibility for providing various public services within the welfare sector. When in power, these non-socialist parties set about demonstrating that fears concerning the dismantling of the welfare state were unfounded.

Though both Denmark and Norway are clearly representative cases of the same politico-economic orientation, there are a few differences worth noting. In Denmark, economic planning and state ownership have never been as extensively practiced as in Norway. And the welfare system in Norway is much more state-oriented than in Denmark, where unions have shared in the responsibility for providing welfare benefits.

Parliamentary Arrangements

Parliaments consist of just one chamber in both Denmark (the Folketing) and Norway (the Storting).[12] And in both countries, the government is based on the parties holding seats in parliament (see Damgaaard 2011; Narud and Strøm 2011). In spite of these basic similarities, there are some relevant differences as well.

The Norwegian parliament is elected for a four-year period and cannot be dissolved, while in Denmark the Folketing can be – and often is – dissolved before a four-year term expires. Thus, between 1945 and 1993, there were thirteen parliamentary elections in Norway and twenty in Denmark. This institutional difference has important consequences for the parties. In periods of coalition governments or single-party minority governments, Norwegian parliamentary parties are to a greater extent forced to cooperate with one another. If a government resigns, other parties have to form a new government based on the same parliament. In contrast, Danish parties and governments can appeal to the electorate to solve political stalemates.

Electoral System and Seat Distribution

The parliaments in both countries are elected by proportional representation, using the modified Saint-Lague formula. Here too, though, there are important differences. First, Norwegian voters can only vote for a party list of candidates but cannot in practice express preferences among the candidates,[13] while Danish voters *must* express a preference for one candidate. As a result, the Norwegian parties have a much tighter grip on the selection of parliamentary candidates than do the Danish parties.

Second, there is a difference in the nature of parliamentary constituencies. All Norwegian seats are allocated to nineteen constituencies which are identical to the provinces, while in Denmark there is a mixture of province-based constituencies and candidate constituencies within provinces.

Finally, in Denmark a party has had to clear a formal 2 per cent hurdle in order to win any seats, while there was, until 1989, no formal hurdle in Norway. Until then, all seats in the Storting were allocated proportionally within provinces. Though no formal hurdle applied, in practice it still required a party whose support was widespread to get nearly 4 per cent of the nationwide vote in order to win a seat.[14] After 1989, revised electoral law provided eight second-tier seats which are allocated to parties whose vote shares deviate most from their seat shares, though a party must win at least 4 per cent of the vote nationwide in order to qualify for any of those seats.[15] So, though there was still no formal hurdle in Norway for the 157 seats distributed proportionally within constituencies, in reality a 4 per cent effective hurdle applied for most seats.[16]

Party Systems

Though the notion of 'the Scandinavian five party model' has always been based at least partly in myth, and certainly fails to describe either the Danish or the Norwegian party system today, it is nevertheless true that these two systems did share a basic form during the formative years of the Progress parties. Both countries had multi-party systems, with the largest parties being the Social Democrats (formally, Labour in Norway) and the Conservatives (formally, the Right in Norway and the Conservative People's Party in Denmark), and with the former as the traditionally leading party.[17] Both countries had distinctly agrarian-based parties (the Liberals in Denmark; the Centre Party in Norway), a Liberal Party (formally, the Radical Liberals in Denmark), a Christian People's Party,[18] and a party to the left of the Social Democrats (Communist/Socialist People's Party).[19]

As of the mid-1970s, both Norway and Denmark had experienced significant new fragmentation of their party systems. Splits and new formations resulted in multiple parties on the left, and in the years leading up to the electoral earthquakes of 1973, several other new parties developed in both countries, including the Progress parties. Supporting prognostications that many of these new formations would fail electorally was the fact that there had not been a recent history of support for fringe parties or movements of either the left or right in either country.[20]

In spite of the basic similarities between the Danish and Norwegian party systems, though, there were also some important contrasts. In relative electoral strength, for instance, Norway's Labour Party had been far more successful than its Danish counterpart (Tables 2.1a and 2.1b). Until 1961 Labour enjoyed majority status in the Storting, something the Danish Social Democrats have never achieved, with obvious consequences for government formation (discussed below). The farmers' party in Denmark (the Liberals) has been much stronger than its Norwegian counterpart, having been more successful in gaining a foothold in urban areas (Christensen 1994; Worre 1979). In the centre of the party spectrum, the Danish Radical Liberals have maintained a foothold while the Norwegian Liberal Party declined from 1965 and lost parliamentary representation in 1985, barely managing to win one seat in 1993, and having since then fluctuated from one election to the next (between two and ten seats).

Until 1967 Norway was unique within Scandinavia in having a Christian People's Party, dating back to 1933. Now similar parties exist in the three other countries – including Denmark since 1970 – though Norway's remains stronger than its Danish counterpart (Bergman and Strøm 2011).

Before and during the Progress parties' formative years, a marked difference existed between the two systems in the extent to which the 'major' parties could claim the lion's share of support. Between 1965 and 1993 the combined strength of the Labour and Conservative parties in Norway ranged between 71.2 per cent (in 1985) and 52.7 per cent (in 1973). In Denmark, the two largest parties during that same period managed a maximum of only 54.5 per cent (in 1968), and their worst combined showing was just 34.8 per cent (in 1973). The poorest performance in both countries came in 1973, but while the Norwegian parties were able to make a quick comeback, it took the two Danish parties ten years to regain their previous strength.

Relative stability gave way to marked change in both party systems in 1973, though to somewhat different degrees. In Denmark, the so-called electoral earthquake of that year produced several new players through splits and new party formations, with the number of parties in parliament jumping from five to ten. At the same time, tremors in Norway raised the number of parliamentary parties from five to eight. Though both systems were clearly receptive to formation of new parties, it would be hard to escape the conclusion that the Danish system was even more open to fragmentation than the Norwegian system was.

Government Formation

The more highly fragmented the party system, the less likely it is that any one party could win enough seats to govern alone, especially with majority status. That general rule, as applied to our two systems, means that single-party government had been even less likely in Denmark than in Norway, and that single-party majority government was less likely in either system after the proliferation of parties in the 1970s than might have been the case earlier.

Indeed, Denmark's 'leading' party – the Social Democratic Party – had always governed either in coalition with others or alone with a minority cabinet, while the Norwegian Labour Party had not been part of a coalition since the pan-political government of 1945 (and would not be again until 2005).[21] And though the Norwegian system had been less fragmented than the Danish, later developments increased fragmentation in Norway, while it decreased in Denmark (Damgaard 2011: 69). With changes in the balance among parties and the emergence of new parties, coalitions and minority governments also became more commonplace in Oslo (see Narud and Strøm 2011).

An interesting and important difference between the two systems, especially from the standpoint of new parties attempting to 'break in', has to do with 'partner loyalty'. Though Labour in Norway never governed in coalition throughout the formative period of the Progress Party, the Conservatives did so with the Liberals, the Christian People's Party, and the Centre Party.[22] In Denmark, on the other hand, the Liberals, the Social Liberals, and the Christians each joined with the Conservatives and – at least once – with the Social Democrats. (See Tables 2.2a and 2.2b.)

Table 2.2a   Danish Governments, 1968–2016

Period	Party Composition	Governing Status
02.Feb.68–11.Oct.71	Rad.Lib., Cons., Lib.	Majority
11.Oct.71–19.Dec.73	Social Democrats	Minority
19.Dec.73–13.Feb.75	Liberals	Minority
13.Feb.75–26.Feb.77	Social Democrats	Minority
26.Feb.77–30.Aug.78	Social Democrats	Minority
30.Aug.78–26.Oct.79	Soc. Dem., Liberals	Minority
26.Oct.79–30.Dec.81	Social Democrats	Minority
30.Dec.81–10.Sept.82	Social Democrats	Minority
10.Sept.82–10.Sept.87	Cons., Lib., Centre, Christian Peoples	Minority
10.Sept.87–03.Jun.88	Cons., Lib., Centre, Christian Peoples	Minority
03.Jun.88–18.Dec.90	Cons., Lib., Rad.Lib.	Minority
18.Dec.90–25.Jan.93	Cons., Lib.	Minority
25.Jan.93–27.Sept.94	Social Democrats, Rad.Lib., Centre, Christian Peoples P.	Majority
27.Sept.94–30.Dec.96	Social Democrats, Rad.Lib., Centre	Minority
30.Dec.96–23.Mar.98	Social Democrats, Rad.Lib.	Minority
23.Mar.98–27.Nov.01	Social Democrats, Rad.Lib.	Minority
27.Nov.01–18.Feb.05	Lib., Con.	Minority
18.Feb.05–23.Nov.07	Lib., Con.	Minority
23.Nov.07–05.Apr.09	Lib., Cons.	Minority
05.Apr.09–03.Oct.11	Lib., Cons.	Minority
03.Oct.11–03.Feb.14	Social Democrats, Rad.Lib., Socialist People's Party	Minority
03.Feb.14–28.Jun.15	Social Democrats,Rad.Lib.	Minority
28.Jun.15–	Lib.	Minority

Source: Damgaard 2011; http://www.ft.dk/folketinget/oplysningen/regeringer/regeringer_siden_1953.aspx

Table 2.2b   Norwegian Governments, 1963–2016

Period	Party Composition	Governing Status
25.Sep.63–12.Oct.65	Labour	Minority
12.Oct.65–17.Mar.71	Centre, Cons., Lib., Christ.	Majority
17.Mar.71–18.Oct.72	Labour	Minority
18.Oct.72–16.Oct.73	Christ., Centre, Lib.	Minority
16.Oct.73–15.Jan.76	Labour	Minority
15.Jan.76–04.Feb.81	Labour	Minority
04.Feb.81–14.Oct.81	Labour	Minority
14.Oct.81–08.Jun.83	Conservative	Minority
08.Jun.85–08.Sep.85	Cons., Lib., Centre	Majority
08.Sep.85–09.May.86	Cons., Lib., Centre	Minority
09.May.86–16.Oct.89	Labour	Minority
16.Oct.89–03.Nov.90	Cons., Lib., Centre	Minority
03.Nov.90–17.Oct.97	Labour	Minority
17.Oct.97–17.Mar.00	Christ., Centre, Lib.	Minority
17.Mar.00–19.Oct.01	Labour	Minority
19.Oct.01–17.Oct.05	Cons., Christ., Lib.	Minority
17.Oct.05–16.Oct.13	Labour, Centre, Soc. Left P.	Majority
16.Oct.13–	Cons., Progress	Minority

Source: http://www.regjeringen.no/nn/om-regjeringa/tidligere/oversikt/ministerier_regjeringer/nyere_tid/
regjeringer.html?id=438715

It is true that in Norway, minority Labour Party governments have benefited from support from the opposition parties – particularly from the parties
in the centre of the system – on an issue-by-issue basis, but not by formal
pact. When the Liberals announced in the 1985 campaign that they would
prefer governing in coalition with Labour to joining the other non-Socialist
parties, the Liberals lost their last two seats. That disaster would be taken as
evidence of the continuing symbolic importance of the cleavage between the
left and the right in Norwegian politics.[23] The evidence seemed to suggest
that both the larger and the smaller parties in Denmark had greater flexibility
in considering coalition partners – perhaps to include new parties – than did
their counterparts in Norway. (This 'common knowledge' would not be challenged until 2005, when Labour not only formed a coalition, but formed one
that included the Centre Party.)[24]

Nature of Established Party Organisations

New parties hoping to succeed electorally must eventually become cogni-
sant of the way the established parties 'do things', whether to emulate or to
reject them. In both Norway and Denmark, the structure of party organisations has tended to reflect the hierarchical system of government, with lay-
ers of regional and municipal governments and party organisations beneath
the national level. And in both countries, parties have traditionally – but

Table 2.3   Cumulated Party Membership in Denmark and Norway, 1960–2012

Year	Denmark	Norway
1960	599,173	376,373
1965	568,412	385,662
1970	473,891	388,179
1975	364,402	360,403
1980	282,420	460,913
1985	274,687	487,194
1990	235,883	427,676
1994	182,876	285,468
2005	176,471	163,810
2012	152,963	163,985

Source: Bille 1992; Svåsand 1992. (Table includes parties as listed in figures 2.1 and 2.2 and includes esti-
mates for missing years. For Norway, collective membership in the Labour Party is included.) Denmark
2005–12: Kosiara-Pedersen 2015. Norway 2005–12: Allern et al. 2016.

in varying ways – been based on mass mobilisation of members and, also
consistent with the 'mass party model', have generally been linked to, or
associated with, organised interests in society (e.g. trade unions and voluntary
organisations) (Allern and Heidar 2001; Bille and Christiansen 2001).

Though, historically speaking, parties in both systems have tended to place
value on membership, Norwegian parties were generally healthier in the 1980s
through early 1990s as membership organisations than the Danish parties (Table
2.3). Danish party membership declined rapidly in the post-earthquake period
(Togeby 1992), but the trend had been evident since 1960. Overall Norwegian
party membership was kept stable (except in the turbulent aftermath of the
1972 EC vote) through at least 1985, in spite of a decline for Labour, largely
because of a massive organisational mobilisation by the Conservative and the
Christian People's parties. Despite a downturn in Norwegian membership in
the late 1980s, the proportion of voters claiming party membership was still
nearly twice as large in Norway as in Denmark, roughly 15 per cent versus
8 per cent. Relatedly, Norwegian parties also tended to retain the loyalty of
their voters longer than was the case for Danish parties (Borre 1992).

To the extent that parties' 'environments' affect their organisation (e.g.
see Harmel and Janda 1982), it is noteworthy that the Danish and Norwegian
environments during the period leading up to and including the early development of the Progress parties shared some relevant features while differing on
others. In both countries, state-run television and radio allocated to all parties equal amounts of time for messages to the public, and the parties could
not purchase time for commercials on television. In Denmark and Norway,
cultural norms stressing cooperation tended to dampen confrontational campaign styles. And in both countries, television was becoming an important
source of information for the voters, increasing the attention paid to central
party leadership.

But the two countries' political environments also differed in two ways which would impact directly on both party campaigns and party organisation. First, Norwegian parties developed more organisational infrastructure in the 1970s after the introduction of general (and generous) public subsidies; Danish parties did not receive such subsidies until 1987.[25] Second, because of the fixed election period, Norwegian political parties were able to plan their campaigns in ways that Danish parties were denied, with implications for strategic planning, platform development, and even the internal power distribution within the parties. As Bille (1991) has noted, Danish parties had to be prepared to run a campaign on short notice and that is the 'single most important factor in understanding Danish election campaigns', undoubtedly contributing (along with Denmark's smaller size) to the greater centralisation of party campaigns in Denmark compared to Norway.

CONCLUSION

Our purpose in this chapter has been to introduce the two Progress parties and their contexts. In the process, it has become apparent that both parties had – by the 1990s – outlived the expectations of many that they would die young, taking their places among the 'flash parties' of history. At their birth, the odds against the institutionalisation of either party might indeed have seemed insurmountable, partly because of their status as entrepreneurial right-wing protest parties, and partly because of their environments. Though we have merely described those contexts here, and have not yet systematically deduced their full relevance for the Progress parties, it is not difficult to infer that some features would hardly be conducive to the success of these new right-wing parties. As parties opposed to organisation (where previously successful parties had shared mass party organisation), opposed to high taxes and big government (where even non-socialist parties had subscribed to the welfare state model), and located on the far-right wings of their party systems (where electoral support had been minimal for fringe parties of any type), the Progress parties would hardly have been expected to achieve the status of institutions. And yet, through processes which we will attempt to describe and explain in the next five chapters, both Progress parties had indeed been institutionalised by the 1990s.

NOTES

1. In May 1972 Glistrup sought – but was denied – nomination to stand in the parliamentary election for the Conservative Party (Hahn-Pedersen 1981: 24–34).
2. The total number of seats in the Folketing was and is 179, but of these four are reserved for Greenland and the Faroe Islands.

3. Glistrup was first found guilty in 1978, but lost his final appeal on 22 June 1983 (Fremskridtspartiet 1996).

4. Only for a few months in the period between 1981 and 1982 did Glistrup hold a formal position – that of political spokesperson for the parliamentary group.

5. In the general election of 1984 Glistrup was reelected to the Folketing, but because he was serving time in prison his election was annulled and his seat assigned to Kjærsgaard, his suppliant.

6. Mogens Glistrup, after being denied nomination for parliament in 1990, founded the Well-being Party but did not succeed in being elected.

7. The full title was '100 gode grunde til et VKZ-flertal' (100 good reasons for a majority of Liberals, Conservatives, and Progress).

8. We will say much more about the post-1995 period in chapter 8.

9. However, when it came time to formalise the position, Lange offered it to Hagen. Hagen insisted that normal bureaucratic procedures should be followed to make it official. Instead, Lange reported to a newspaper that Hagen would now become general secretary 'over my dead body' (Hagen 2007: 48–50, 54–55).

10. Karl Almas, who had been elected in 1973 as a Progress Party member of parliament but who had shared Hagen's views about party organisation, split and founded the Reform Party in July of 1974. When Lange passed away on 18 October 1974, Hagen replaced him in parliament and joined Almas in the Reform Party (Iversen 1998: 60–61).

11. The latter established a separate political organization, but stopped short of forming a party.

12. While the Storting is elected as one chamber, until 2009 the Norwegian parliament was divided into two separate chambers after the election for the purpose of passing legislation. In practical terms this arrangement did not matter as the political parties were proportionally represented in both chambers.

13. Norwegian voters *may* express a preference for a candidate on the party list of their choice. However, for the preference to have any effect on the ranking of the candidates, more than half of the voters for that party must indicate a similar preference. Thus, in reality, preference voting has no effect in Norway. The Norwegian ballot is therefore considered to be a fixed ballot.

14. Of course, a party could win a seat with a smaller proportion of the vote if its support was concentrated in one region of the country. This, for instance, enabled the Red Electoral Alliance to win representation from the Oslo constituency even though its share of the nationwide vote was far less than 4 per cent.

15. As of 2001, the number of second-tier seats has been nineteen.

16. As of 2001, this statement has still applied but for 150 seats distributed proportionally within districts.

17. More recently, it has been the case in Denmark that the Liberals have surpassed the Conservatives as the second-largest party or ruled as a single-party minority government (2015–2017). And beginning in 2001, the Liberals have at times been the largest party in parliament. In Norway, it is the Progress Party itself which has surpassed the Conservatives in three of the five recent elections beginning in 1997.

18. Though originally labelled the Christian People's Party, the name in English was officially changed to Christian Democrats in 2003.

19. Prior to the 1960s, the Communist Party was the only party to the left of the Social Democrats. Since the 1961 election the Communists disappeared and the Socialist People's Party (SF) became the left-wing alternative. SF was replaced in 1975 by an electoral alliance, SV, consisting of the former SF along with the defectors from the Communist Party and some independent socialists. The alliance was formalised as a unified new party (SV) in 1978.

20. In the inter-war period, fascist parties had failed electorally (Lindstrøm 1985), and in the post-war period support for the Communist parties had declined rapidly as the Cold War period developed.

21. The Norwegian Labour Party did enter government in coalition in 2005.

22. However, not *all four* parties have participated in *all* the coalition governments; see table 2.2b.

23. The so-called Red-Green coalition between the Socialist Left, the Labour Party and the Centre Party established in 2005 is the first instance of a coalition government bridging the traditional gap between socialist and non-socialist parties.

24. Hence, it is particularly ironic that it is in Norway, not Denmark, that Progress was able to break into government (in 2013), while the Danish People's Party has not yet done so.

25. Though subsidies for Denmark's parliamentary parties were introduced in 1965, the extra-parliamentary organisations began receiving state subventions in 1987. In Norway, subventions to the parliamentary parties began in 1966, though subsidies to the extra-parliamentary organisations were first disbursed in 1970.

Part II

INSTITUTIONALISATION

Chapter 3

Party Institutionalisation

Concepts and Indicators

In chapters 1 and 2 we have alluded to predictions that the Progress parties would die young, certainly short of becoming 'institutions'. In chapter 5, we will explore in much more detail the combination of extant literature and specific circumstances which gave rise to such predictions. But here in chapter 3 it is our purpose to develop the concepts and indicators with which to assess the extent to which – and the ways in which – a party has in fact institutionalised. In chapter 4 we will apply this framework to each of the two Progress parties.

It is our primary contention in this chapter that the building of theory on institutionalisation of political parties[1] (and political organisations more generally) can be substantially enhanced by recognising that 'institutionalisation' is a multidimensional concept whose individual components are theoretically related, but not conceptually redundant. Recognising that institutionalisation has more than one dimension should not only help theory building by clarifying the meaning(s) of the concept itself, but may also serve to expand the search for explanatory variables, since the different dimensions may indeed be best explained by different types or levels of factors.[2]

APPROACHES TO INSTITUTIONALISATION
IN THE EXISTING LITERATURE

A number of approaches to institutionalisation have been applied in the study of political parties. We begin here with four 'classical approaches' (Huntington 1968; Janda 1980; Panebianco 1988; and Rose and Mackie 1988) that are commonly cited or used by others, then consider a number of more recent treatments, and finally offer our own.

The definition of institutionalisation that is most often used throughout political science is that of Samuel Huntington, who sees it as 'the process by which organisations and procedures acquire value and stability' (12). From that definition, he argues that institutionalisation may be measured 'by its adaptability, complexity, autonomy, and coherence' (12). Huntington's approach has been used primarily in the study of political change, and especially the modernisation of societies, but has also been applied to the study of political parties (see Formisano 1974; Polsby 1968; Wellhofer 1972). The central component of this approach is *time*, that is, the ability of a structure to survive and to achieve stability so that its existence is not totally dependent upon its original members and leaders.

Panebianco (1988) further developed the concept, specifically for use in the study of parties. Defining institutionalisation as 'the way the organisation "solidifies"' (49), Panebianco argues for measuring along two scales: '(1) that of the organisation's degree of autonomy vis-a-vis its environment, and (2) that of its degree of systemness, i.e. the degree of interdependence of its different internal sectors' (55). The latter scale is further defined as 'the internal structural coherence of the organisation' (56), maintained by 'centralised control of organisational resources and exchange processes with the environment'. More specifically, five indicators of degree of party institutionalisation are suggested and considered:

(1) degree of development of the central extra-parliamentary organisation ... ,
(2) degree of homogeneity of organisational structures at the same hierarchical level ... ,
(3) how the organisation is financed ... ,
(4) relations with the external collateral organisations ... , [and]
(5) degree of correspondence between a party's statutory norms and its 'actual power structure ... ' (58–59).

In effect, then, for Panebianco institutionalisation includes organisational complexity, autonomy, internal cohesiveness, and a centralised authority pattern (on the last, see esp. 56–57).

In their treatment of institutionalisation, both Huntington and Panebianco emphasise organisational attributes, and both include within their indicators several which might be thought of as conceptually distinct from, though perhaps causally related to, the authors' narrower initial definitions of institutionalisation. Janda (1980), for instance, explicitly treats concepts like autonomy as related to, but not part of, institutionalisation.[3] He notes that 'a party can be highly institutionalised and yet lack independence of other groups (Huntington's "autonomy") – as [with] the Labour Party in Great Britain' (19). The same argument would seem to hold, in the main, for organisational complexity, centralisation of power, and internal coherence, all of which Janda treats as separate concepts throughout his own cross-national parties project.

Janda himself defines an institutionalised party as 'one that is reified in the public mind so that "the party" exists as a social organisation apart from its momentary leaders, and this organisation demonstrates recurring patterns of behaviour valued by those who identify with it' (19). He then operationalises institutionalisation with six variables: the year of origin, name changes, organisational discontinuity (i.e. splits and mergers), leadership competition, legislative instability, and electoral instability. Thus, Janda's approach seemingly recognises not just an internal, organisational component of institutionalisation, but what might be considered an 'external' component as well. While 'leadership competition' clearly indicates internal routinisation of leadership selection, legislative and electoral instability tap a different, external dimension: treatment of the party as an 'institution' by the electorate.[4] (More later on the relationship of the other indicators to the broader concept!)

Richard Rose and Thomas Mackie (1988) take a 'minimalist' approach to both conceptualising and measuring institutionalisation of parties. To become institutionalised is, for them, 'to merit recognition as an established party'. While doing so requires three things ('[1] create cross-local organisation to contest elections nationwide; [2] nominate candidates to fight national elections; and [3] continue to nominate candidates at successive elections'[535]), only one indicator is employed in Rose and Mackie's own analysis:

> An institutionalised party must continue from election to election; operationally a party is judged to have become institutionalised if it fights more than three national elections. A group that fails to do this is not an established political party, but an ephemeral party. (536)

The Huntington and Panebianco approaches emphasise internal, organisational aspects of institutionalisation to the exclusion of 'external' perceptions of the party as institution; Rose and Mackie emphasise the latter to the exclusion of the former; Janda includes some of both.

More recent approaches to party institutionalisation continue to incorporate some of the 'classical' elements while introducing some new ones. Veugelers (1995: 4), as quoted in Pedahzur and Brichta (2002: 35), defines

> institutionalisation as a combination of systemic, temporal, spatial criteria of party success: (a) a party has systemic importance if it has governing or blackmail potential; (b) a party has temporal importance if it persists without interruption – a stable party fields candidates in successive national elections; (c) a party has spatial importance if it pervades the polity – a national party fields candidates across the country.

Thus, Veugelers adds national scope and perceived importance by other parties (as presumably would be required for governing or blackmail potential) to the more traditional element of persistence over time.[5]

Levitsky (1998) emphasises two dimensions: 'value infusion' and 'behavioural routinisation', arguing that the two should be treated separately rather than combined. For Levitsky, value infusion occurs when a party, in Janda's terms, 'is reified in the public mind' or, in Huntington's terms, is 'valued for itself' rather than its original purposes or goals. As an example, he offers evidence of the Peronist leaders and members remaining committed 'through periods of severe diversity and despite important changes in the organisation's goals and strategies' (82), including Peron's death. As for routinisation, he argues that prior literature recognising only routinisation into formal rules had been mistaken; routinisation of informal patterns of behaviour should count as well.

Defining the process of institutionalisation of a new party as 'the transformation of the party from a mere instrument of founders for the pursuit of a set of goals in its formative phase into "an end in itself" for the majority of supporters later on', and following Levitsky (1998) and Randall and Svåsand (2002), Bolleyer (2013: 55–56) also adopts the dual *internal party life* dimensions of value infusion and routinisation.

Pedahzur and Brichta (2002) also employ a two-pronged approach, starting with Rose and Mackie's operationalisation as persistence, but broadening it beyond just the more-than-three-elections rule: 'Even though [their] definition does not allow us to judge whether one party is more institutionalised than the other, we may assume that the more elections the party contests the more institutionalised it becomes'. They go on to add the elements of electoral and legislative stability, as had been included in Janda's approach.

Finally, Arter and Kestila-Kekkonen (2014) adopt a multidimensional approach with the dimensions defined by different venues:

> an institutionalised party will have a stable electoral base – that is, a body of 'core supporters' (societal rootedness); the electoral party will be served by an organisational structure having a core membership, an effective candidate supply and a *de facto* dispersal of roles and authority (autonomy and systemness); and its body of elected representatives will function as a coherent legislative actor (cohesion) and, if and when necessary, sustain the party in government. (937)

They then add 'adaptability' as well. Thus, their approach incorporates a stable support base, persistent electoral participation, internal routinisation, legislative cohesion, and adaptability. For them, institutionalisation does not necessarily occur simultaneously in the electoral, organisational, and legislative arenas.

It is obvious from this inventory of others' approaches that institutionalisation means many different things to many different folks. While our own approach incorporates many of the elements just discussed, it stops far short of including all of them. While it joins other approaches in being multidimensional, the dimensions are not exactly the same as for any of the others.

OUR APPROACH

Our approach is rooted in consideration of the major roles that the concept of institutionalisation has played in the development of theory concerning political parties. In our understanding of the literature, there are three such roles:

1. as an internally institutionalised organisation, valued in its own right and with the organisation and its personnel behaving accordingly;
2. as perceptions by other actors – external to the party itself – that the party is an 'institution' to be counted upon, taken into account, and/or reckoned with for the foreseeable future; and
3. as an objectively durable organisation, which has long persisted in spite of difficulties and 'shocks'.

Our conceptual approach, then, recognises three separate dimensions (or 'types') of party institutionalisation, distinguished by 'role' more so than venue:

1. as internal behaviour indicative of reification of the party aside from its founding leaders and their initial goals ('internal' or 'organisational' institutionalisation), as demonstrated in routinised organisational behaviour and non-personalisation of internal party loyalty (i.e. value infusion);
2. as the perception, and consequent behaviour, by other actors that the party has 'lasting power' ('external' or 'perceptual' institutionalisation);[6] and
3. as an objectively established survival record, that is, objective durability ('objective' institutionalisation).

And our approach to operationalisation must also reflect all three dimensions:

1. evidence of ability to adjust to changing goals and purposes for the party as well as routinisation of decision-making processes, including but not limited to leadership selection, in ways which suggest that the party can have a 'life of its own' beyond the political lives and goals of its current leader(s),

2. evidence that the party has become part of the 'routines' of other relevant actors in ways which suggest that they consider it to be an 'established party', to borrow Rose and Mackie's terminology, and
3. a record of durability that includes both persistence and ability to survive shocks.

While all three dimensions are necessary for achieving what we label 'institutionhood' – the state of being fully institutionalised – each of the separate dimensions also has value in its own right for measuring and theorising about institutionalisation, as will be argued more elaborately below.

Having established what *is* included in our conceptualisation of institutionalisation, we should make clear what it does *not* include. While the approaches of Huntington, Panebianco, and Arter and Kestila-Kekkonen all include at least some external autonomy, organisational complexity, centralisation of power, and internal cohesion, we join with Janda in treating those concepts as separate from institutionalisation. Institutionalised parties can come in many forms, including externally autonomous or dependent;[7] organisationally complex or simple; centralised or decentralised; and cohesive or factionalised.[8] And while Veugelers requires national scope, we see no reason for assuming the non-institutionalisability of regional or local parties. Institutionalisation and each of these other concepts may be related theoretically, but they are – and should be kept – conceptually distinct.

Though we agree with Janda's exclusions in his conceptual approach to institutionalisation, we disagree with two of his specific indicators. Among his six indicators, he includes 'name changes' and 'organisational discontinuity'. Janda sees name change as an indicator of *lack* of institutionalisation of the party, since it may be 'assumed to result in at least momentary confusion about the party's identity within the citizenry at large'. But some name changes could in fact *increase* the institutionalisation of the party, indicating its maturity rather than its instability (as we feel is the case of the Norwegian Progress Party, formerly known as Anders Lange's Party for a Drastic Reduction in Taxes, Rates, and Public Intervention). This is even more clearly the case when parties that have existed for a long time nevertheless see fit to change their name, as did the agrarian parties in Sweden (1957) and in Norway (1959). These parties' changes to the 'Centre Party' label are best seen as organisational adaptation to changing environments, that is, with declining numbers in the agricultural sector (Christensen 1994).

Likewise, organisational discontinuities in the forms of splits or mergers *may* (as Janda argues) alter the 'interaction patterns' by narrowing/broadening the party's focus, or even bring about the end of the party. If the party can endure such discontinuities, however, the end result may in fact be a stronger party internally which is perceived as a more viable institution externally, and which has given a clear indication of its durability.[9]

The fact that Janda's own factor analysis showed name changes and organisational discontinuities to have low inter-correlations with his other four indicators is not surprising in this light. Hence, we think it more reasonable to treat name changes and organisational discontinuities as factors *in* institutionalisation than as indicators *of* its opposite.

We turn now to a detailed examination of each of the three dimensions that *are* included in institutionalisation.

INTERNAL INSTITUTIONALISATION

Internal institutionalisation refers to behaviour and attitudes *within the organisation* that are indicative of reification – 'in the party's own mind' – of the party aside from the founder or any particular leaders or purposes of the moment. As such, internal institutionalisation itself is two-dimensional, encompassing both (1) the routinisation (e.g. de-personalisation) of decision-making procedures and (2) the behaviour of internal party actors – including members and public office holders – indicative of attaching value to the party rather than just to temporary leaders or ambitions of the moment (i.e. 'internal value infusion').

Routinisation

'Routinisation' of parties' internal behaviour has been considered a key organisational element for distinguishing 'charismatic' parties, reliant on one *person*, from parties with more 'normal' organisational structures reliant on *rules and procedures* rather than on a single, omniscient and omnipotent, personality. Panebianco, for instance, distinguishes between the party organisation 'founded exclusively on personal ties' (the 'charismatic' party) from those based on '"rules", internal "career patterns", and a clear division of labour' (143–144). More generally speaking, routinisation is the dimension of institutionalisation most clearly and directly linked to Huntington's definition as 'stable, valued, recurring patterns of behaviour' and Janda's criterion that 'this organisation demonstrates recurring patterns of behaviour valued by those who identify with it' (both in Janda 1980: 19). Levitsky (1998) also treats routinisation as a key component of institutionalisation, arguing explicitly for incorporating 'informally routinized behaviour patterns' as well as routinisation in conformity with formal rules. Seen in this way, routinisation can be demonstrated by two kinds of evidence:

1. *written rules* that are perceived as legitimate by party leaders as well as the membership; there is expectation that they will be followed, and
2. *actual behaviour* suggestive of regularised behaviour, whether rules are written or not; this amounts to de-personalisation of the party.

Though written rules would not be sufficient evidence of routinisation in the absence of the actual behaviour for older parties, of course, the first criterion (including the expectation of compliance) is all that could reasonably be expected for some parties too new to have demonstrated 'recurring patterns of behaviour' in practice.[10]

On the other hand, some more mature parties may have developed recurring patterns of behaviour and expectations even in the absence of a written and formally adopted set of rules (e.g. the Peronists, as analysed by Levitsky 1998). The British Conservative Party, for instance, did not have any *formal* rules for leadership selection prior to 1965 (Punnett 1992). When was a leadership change it was referred to as 'the emergence of the party leader'.[11] But it would not be correct to infer from a missing formal rule on leadership election that the British Conservative Party was not following routinised behaviour patterns before 1965.

So while it is possible – and our conceptualisation allows – for routinisation to take place in the absence of formalisation of rules, it is certainly easier to detect when rules are indeed both formalised and followed. Even when a party does have what constitute formalised party statutes covering such things as leadership selection, candidate nomination, and party finances, it is still possible of course for those rules to be altered over time. The key feature of *change* in such cases, though, is whether the party change itself is made following procedures outlined in the statutes and known to the participants in the party. In other words, in an institutionalised party, change does not occur at the whim of a party leader. With this in mind, an important indicator of routinisation in a party with formalised rules is that when those rules are changed, the changes are made following steps specified in the party's statutes.

For parties whose routinisation of behaviour patterns is of the less formal variety, a similar criterion should apply. That is, the routinised patterns should not be changed willy-nilly, by means that themselves are not included in the routinised, albeit informal, patterns of behaviour.

Whether routinisation is by formal or informal means, it is a truism that there is no party with a perfect match between the rules/patterns and how the party operates in practice. But in the routinised party, those rules/patterns are more, rather than less, accepted and followed in practice. And when a practice deviates from the norms, there should nevertheless be a sense of legitimacy, that is, general acceptance that the deviating practices serve to supplement, but not replace, the rules/patterns which the party has adopted (Helmke and Levitsky 2004).

Internal Value Infusion

As indicated above, the concept of 'value infusion' has elsewhere been equated with a party becoming 'valued for itself' rather than just its leaders, and becoming 'an end in itself' beyond its original goals and purposes (Bolleyer 2013; Levitsky 1998). Seznick suggests that value infusion occurs

> when an organisation becomes 'infused with value beyond the technical requirement of the task at hand, or when actors' goals shift from the pursuit of particular objectives *through* the organisation to the goal of perpetuating the organisation per se. (Selznick, 1957: 17, cited in Levitsky 1998: 79)

When sometimes treated as akin to 'reification in the public mind', the concept could take on an 'external' aspect, with the 'valuing' being done by the electorate (and indeed resulting in a stable long-term party electorate).[12] For our purposes here, though, 'internal value infusion' refers explicitly to reification in the 'party's own mind', that is in the collective and individual minds of its members, elected officials, and other party personnel.

The extent that internal party actors demonstrate allegiance to the party itself, separately from any particular leader(s) or special ambitions of the moment, indicates that the party is being valued for itself, in its own right. Development of a stable membership base and minimal defections of party representatives could be taken as specific indicators of internal value infusion. Rampant resignations and/or party-switching by elected representatives or party members – particularly after the departure of a particular leader – would presumably indicate the opposite.

Though we consider routinisation and value infusion to be different and separable dimensions of the more general concept of 'internal institutionalisation' (as do Bolleyer 2013 and Levitsky 1998), we nonetheless recognise that in some instances successful routinisation may in fact serve as an indicator of internal value infusion. In those cases where development of 'normal', routinised party organisation was not an objective of the party's founders – who in fact may have seen normal organisation and even institutionalisation more generally as faults to be avoided – successful routinisation could well be taken as evidence of the party having moved on from those founders and their original purposes and ambitions for the party.

EXTERNAL INSTITUTIONALISATION

'External institutionalisation' consists of perceptions by others that the party is indeed an 'institution', and is to be thought of and treated as such. These external perceptions have at least two major components: the party's *perceived* 'lasting power' and its *perceived* 'relevance'. For the relevant external actor (whether a potential voter or another party's leader), a reasonable question would be 'Is this a party whose presence should cause me to rethink my own behaviour?', or 'Is it relevant to me, and is it likely to be around long enough that I should care?' If the answers are 'yes', then for that external actor, the party is perceived to be an institution (and may affect that actor's behaviour accordingly), regardless of the new party's levels of persistence or internal routinisation. The most relevant actors asking such questions, from the standpoint of the new party, would seem to be (1) the electorate and (2) the other parties.

Indicators of these actors' perceptions of the new party may come in two forms: (1) direct evidence of the attitudes of voters (or leaders of the other parties) and (2) evidence of their altered behaviour as a consequence of the new party's presence in the system. On the part of the electorate, external institutionalisation could be seen in the development of a stable core electorate for the new party (also part of Arter and Kestila-Kekkonen's [2014] 'societal rootedness'), especially when it consists of voters whose reasons for supporting the party indicate the likelihood of continued support.[13] Leaders of other parties might demonstrate their perceptions of the new party directly in statements to the media, or indirectly by altering their own programmes or in other ways indicating enhanced blackmail or coalition potential of the new party (see also Veugelers' [1995] 'systemic performance').[14]

Because it is unreasonable to expect that *all* other parties will perceive the lasting power and/or relevance of the new party in the same way, the perceptions must be weighed by the number and importance of the parties holding them. (At a minimum, only the perceptions of parties which themselves hold at least minimal relevance in the system should be considered.)

OBJECTIVE DURABILITY

Whereas routinisation refers to organisational matters, value infusion taps an internal attitudinal dimension, and external institutionalisation refers to perceptions by outside actors; 'objective durability' may be thought of as an objective estimate of the probability of continued survival of a party, based on its past history of endurance. Existing literature has already established that simply the current age, or what we will call 'persistence', of a party is itself closely related to the likelihood of surviving longer. Janda and Gillies (1980), for instance, studied the survival patterns of 208 parties, and concluded:

> Obviously, there is some analogy to infant mortality in the case of parties as well as humans. Once parties are allowed to mature, their chances of survival increase dramatically. ... For parties between 5 and 15 years of age,

more than sixty percent died before 1979. If a party survives until age 15, its chances of continuing nearly double. After parties reach 25, the probability of continuing jumps to 80 percent. ... It is clear that party longevity, unlike human longevity, is associated with increased likelihood of survival. (166–167)[15]

Clearly, though, persistence alone is not sufficient as a predictor of further survival (particularly in the lower age range), nor as a complete measure of objective durability. The concept of 'durability' includes not just persistence, but also a record of being able to survive 'shocks'[16] (i.e. important changes within the party or in its environment).

We have adapted our own two-pronged approach from Gurr's study of the durability of political systems (1974). For Gurr (and for us), *persistence* 'is defined simply as longevity', while *adaptability* refers 'to the extent of ... demonstrated capacity for undergoing incremental change' (1484). Both aspects would be required for *durability*.

While we agree with Gurr's general approach, we differ by replacing adaptability with *survivability* as the second prong. The word 'adaptability' implies that the party (or in Gurr's case, polity) plays an active role in its own survival, that is, that the party changes something about itself in order to better fit its changed circumstances and/or environment. Webster's dictionary,[17] for instance, says adaptability means to 'adjust oneself to new or changed circumstances' and *Merriam-Webster* defines adaptable as 'able to change or be changed in order to fit or work better in some situation or for some purpose'. We prefer the more general concept of 'survivability', implying ability to withstand shocks, whether due to intentional adaptation or some other factor(s). BusinessDictionary.com defines survivability as the 'capability of a system or organisation to withstand a disaster or hostile environment, without significant impairment of its normal operations', and that is how we use the term here.[18]

As an empirical matter, then, evidence of durability is sought on two dimensions: (1) persistence of a party over a period of time and (2) survivability as shown in its ability to withstand (i.e. 'survive') shocks. A party which is relatively young, but which has already survived many shocks, has thereby provided evidence of durability (i.e. in the aspect of survivability) in spite of its relative youth (i.e. lack of persistence, so far). An old party which has never experienced a shock, on the other hand, has never had the opportunity to demonstrate that it can successfully 'survive'. Hence, a party with both persistence and a record of survivability would attain the highest level of durability. A party with one but not both of the criteria would attain a lower level, though higher than a party with neither age nor a record of survivability.

While the measurement of persistence (i.e. simply the age of the party) is straightforward and poses no problem for our analysis of change in the parties,[19] survivability requires historical analysis of shocks experienced by the parties during their lifetimes. Such shocks might include leadership changes, name changes, 'organisational discontinuities' (i.e. splits, resignations, etc.), and 'environmental changes' such as adjustments in other parties' programmes to neutralise the target party's message. To the extent that even a new party has had such experiences and survived them, it will have demonstrated significant objective durability.[20]

THE ARGUMENT FOR A
MULTIDIMENSIONAL APPROACH

If all parties at a particular level on one dimension of institutionalisation were at similar levels on the others, then this effort to separate the dimensions, conceptually, would be pointless, empirically. But this is not the case. In Norway alone, the Norwegian Communist Party had durability, value infusion, and routinisation, but after the 1970s few voters and no other parties paid much attention to it (i.e. it lacked external institutionalisation on the dimension of 'relevance'); the Pensioners' Party has had durability but no routinisation (disputes over who is actually the party's leader are common) or external institutionalisation. Elsewhere, some of the new environmental parties lack routinisation and a record of durability (being very new), but circumstances could still warrant high expectations that they will last and gain relevance, thus already affecting the behaviour of others. And, according to Panebianco's study of charismatic parties, some parties of that type have established records of durability and external perceptions of relevance, but little or no routinisation or value infusion.

These examples demonstrate why it is necessary, for a thorough treatment of party institutionalisation, to consider all three dimensions: durability plus internal and external institutionalisation. It would be incorrect to assume that evidence of a high (or low) level of institutionalisation on one dimension means the same level of institutionalisation across the board, with consequences for both theory building and predictive ability.[21]

THEORETICAL IMPLICATIONS

While the three dimensions or 'types' of institutionalisation are conceptually and theoretically distinct, they are nonetheless conceptually *related* – through their obvious association with the more general concept of 'institutionalisation' – and they are highly likely to be theoretically related as well. And yet those anticipated theoretical relationships are not so robust as to suggest that the conceptual distinctions are unnecessary. An objective record of durability is likely to contribute to the perception that a party is an 'institution' to be reckoned with, for instance, though some parties are able to reach external institutionalisation even before establishing a record of objective durability. Routinisation and value infusion may be necessary for some parties to be seen by others as predictable and trustworthy, though some highly routinised and value-infused parties may still find it very difficult to achieve external institutionalisation. Internal institutionalisation – especially for parties that were formerly personalistic vehicles – may be necessary for persisting and surviving to a record of objective durability, though party reification by itself may not be sufficient to assure reaching that status. And so on! While one type of institutionalisation may be either necessary or sufficient for another, none is both necessary and sufficient, as would be required for the conceptual distinctions to be empirically and theoretically unnecessary.

While those inter-dimensional relationships are important for understanding why some parties fully institutionalise when others do not, a more complete understanding certainly must include other factors as well.[22] Some of the other concepts of 'party organisation' which we earlier separated from the concept of institutionalisation – for example, organisational complexity, centralisation of party power, and cohesion – may well relate theoretically to one or another of the three types of institutionalisation. Some minimal level of organisational complexity may be necessary for routinisation, for instance; and extreme decentralisation and lack of cohesion could hamper external institutionalisation at the national level.[23] Beyond the party's own organisation, a significant *level* of electoral performance – as distinguished from the electoral *stability* which we associate with the concept of external institutionalisation itself – may well be a contributing factor to internal value infusion, external institutionalisation, and/or objective durability, at least for parties for whom electoral success is the primary goal. And features of the electoral system may also matter; public subsidies, for instance, should make it easier for parties to institutionalise, especially if they would otherwise have had to rely on one or a few private donors for financial sustenance (and hence the possibility of personalisation).[24]

Looking within the party itself, we will in chapter 6 formulate the argument that parties with personal, entrepreneurial roots require different types of leadership skills at three separate phases of the institutionalisation process. Parties whose leaders at one of those stages lack the necessary skills and orientations may well be hampered from institutionalising. On the other hand, prospects for institutionalisation – whether of the external perception or internal varieties – could be markedly enhanced by transfer of leadership from one who resists institutionalisation to one who is determined to pursue institutionalisation.

While all of those may indeed be factors in the explanation for variant experiences with institutionalisation, it is important to recognise that not all such factors will necessarily play the same role. Some may be *triggering* factors, making it more likely that institutionalisation will be pursued. Change from an organisation-resisting leader[25] to one bent on developing more 'normal' party organisation would be such an event. Some may be *hindering* factors. Persistence in top leadership positions by founders who never intended to build anything other than personalistic vehicles, and who consistently and actively resist efforts at routinisation, would be such a hindrance. And some are *favouring conditions*, providing resources needed for institutionalisation should there be motivation and willingness for doing so. An example might be public subsidies, for reasons just noted above.

NOTES

1. Note that this book is about *party* institutionalisation, not the institutionalisation of *party systems*. While these two concepts overlap, and may be theoretically linked, they are not the same thing. Thus, in our references to literature, we will focus upon those pieces which relate directly to party institutionalisation, and will effectively exclude references to literature on institutionalisation of party systems. Note also that while much of our conceptualization and theorizing are broadly applicable to parties and party systems of various sizes and types, our primary focus is upon parties which tend to develop in established multi-party systems prone to generating electoral alliances and/or coalition governments.

2. We will put off treating the concept of de-institutionalisation, which we see as an extension of institutionalisation, to chapter 8.

3. Other authors who do include at least some version of autonomy in their conceptualisation of institutionalisation include Randall and Svåsand (2002) and Basedau and Stroh (2008).

4. While recognizing both of what we have called the internal and external components of institutionalisation, however, Janda proceeds to otherwise treat the two dimensions as though they were one. Beyond the statement of the definition, there is no further mention of the *two* aspects of the concept, though the set of indicators does include measures of both.

5. Lupu (2009) also includes nationalisation as an element of institutionalisation: 'Parties that are more institutionalized should have coherent organizations that are able to penetrate politics broadly' (4). To Lupu, nationalisation is a proxy for organisational institutionalisation (2).

6. This is essentially the same concept as Randall and Svåsand's (2002) 'reification'.

7. Pedahzur and Brichta (2002: 33, 35) have also gone on record as preferring to treat autonomy as a separate concept rather than as a component of institutionalisation.

8. That there are attributes of the internal workings of the party which do indicate internal institutionalisation cannot be denied, however. Some minimal levels of organisational complexity and coherence must be present in order to establish 'routine patterns of behaviour', the essential ingredient for institutions (internally speaking, of course).

9. And in the case of splits, the *type* of split that occurred is likely to be more important than the fact that a split did occur. For instance, if the splitting group is a relatively small component of the parent party and/or if it is on the party's ideological extreme, any negative impact may be negligible.

10. It is important to recognise also that not all departures from formal rules are of the same type, and not all will have the same impact on institutionalisation. There are times, for instance, when parties deviate from the rules in order to avoid a worse outcome, such as a split or a threat to the party's existence. In 1989, for instance, the Norwegian Labour Party changed its statutes to allow for electing two deputy leaders rather than just one. The change was made at the national convention, in spite of a similar proposal which had been rejected at a meeting of the party's national council one year earlier. The change also violated the party's statutes that such changes must be proposed weeks ahead of the convention. The motivation for the change was to avoid a serious division in the party, which could indeed have triggered de-institutionalisation (see Skjeie 1999: 61).

11. Punnett (1992) cites characterisations of the selection 'method' as: 'a procedure of a confidential and mysterious character', 'a magic circle of people close to the Prime Minister', and 'the informal alchemy of a charmed circle of elders' (32–33).

12. As such, 'external value infusion' is reflected in our treatment of 'external institutionalisation' below.

13. Note that the emphasis here is upon electoral *stability* rather than electoral *strength*. A party with a small, but stable, support base is just as institutionalised as one with a stable and large support base. An example is the Norwegian Communist Party. This party, formed in 1921, continues to exist. It holds regular meetings according to its statutes, elects party leaders and nominates candidates for elections, but it has failed to win a single seat in parliament since 1957 (http://nkp.no). Its failure to win seats since 1957 does not mean that it is no longer institutionalised. As a reverse example, the Danish Progress Party became the second-largest party in its debut election in Denmark in 1973, just a few months after it had been formally established. The electoral success did not, at that time, match any criterion for party institutionalisation.

14. The emphasis on a *stable core* electorate disqualifies 'flash' parties from being considered institutionalised on this dimension.

15. Bolleyer (2014: 2) found that 65 of 140 parties formed since 1968 had ceased to persist by the end of 2011. According to Lowery et al., of a total of 161 different parties competing in Dutch elections between 1946 and 2006, 117 (72.67 per cent) competed in only one election (Lowery et al. 2013: 388).

16. We should note we are using the word 'shock' somewhat more liberally here than Harmel and Janda do in their 'Integrated Theory of Party Goals and Party Change' (1994), where a shock is an external stimulus impacting directly upon the party's primary goal. Here we are including both internal and external shocks, and the external variety need not impact upon the 'primary' goal of the party (though 'issues'

were the Progress parties' primary goals throughout the period of our study, with 'votes' being secondary goals, and all of the external stimuli mentioned here would have impacted upon one or the other of those goals).

17. *Webster's New World College Dictionary*. 2010. Fourth edition, Cleveland: Wiley Publishing, Inc.

18. 'Resilience' (Arter 2016) is another option that was considered. Unlike adaptability, resilience does not imply that a party has changed in order to survive. To the contrary, resilience would assume that the party after the shock was essentially the same as before the shock. *Merriam-Webster* (www.merriam-webster.com), for instance, defines 'resilience' as 'the capability of a strained body to recover its size and shape after deformation caused especially by compressive stress' and *The Free Dictionary* (www.thefreedictionary.com) defines it as 'the property of a material that enables it to resume its original shape or position'. Because parties may or may not change in response to shocks, the change-neutral concept of 'survivability' is to be preferred over either adaptability or resilience.

19. While we measure persistence simply as number of years of existence as a party, others would use the number of elections in which the party has participated. Rose and Mackie (1968), for instance, operationalise an institutionalised party as one that has participated in more than three consecutive national elections. Pedahzur and Brichta (2002) use number of elections as a continuous indicator of degree of institutionalisation. Arter and Kestila-Kekkonen (2014) use a different elections-based indicator: a regular supply of candidates. Our approach explicitly allows for parties which only nominally participate in elections, for example, many institutionalised minor parties in the United States.

20. It might be argued that persistence and especially survivability also indirectly indicate that a party 'is reified in the public mind' (Janda 1980) and is 'valued for itself' (Huntington 1968), that is, that they are also indirect indicators of 'value infusion' (Levitsky 1998).

21. Levitsky (1998: 78, 82) clearly agrees. In arguing for treating his two dimensions of value infusion and behavioural routinisation separately, he suggests 'failure to make these conceptual distinctions may pose serious problems for causal analysis'.

22. Because some of the potential factors may be situation-specific, as when explanation for parties in competitive systems differs from that for non-competitive parties in single-party systems, we should be clear that we speak in these pages primarily for the former rather than the latter.

23. In discussing what she sees as 'challenges of institutionalisation', Bolleyer (2013: 72–73) can be seen as alluding to the potentially negative reaction to lack of party cohesion 'from the voters' perspective' and negative implications of decentralisation for establishing national-level routinisation.

24. An extreme case of this may result when a founding leader is him/herself the primary – or perhaps even sole – source of party funds. Such is illustrated by Berlusconi, for instance.

25. Bolleyer (2013: 53–54) also notes this general reluctance of party founders to build institutionalised parties.

Chapter 4

Levels of Party Institutionalisation

The Progress Parties

In chapter 3 we developed a framework of concepts and indicators with which to gauge the extent to which – and the ways in which – a party has institution-alised. In this chapter our purpose is to apply that three-pronged framework in assessing the extent and ways in which each of the Progress parties did *in fact* institutionalise. After discussing, for both parties, the dimension of objective durability (treating separately its components of persistence and survivabil-ity) we move on to discussing the parties' levels of internal and then external institutionalisation.

OBJECTIVE DURABILITY

Persistence

Many Danish politicians back in 1973 expected the party system to return to its traditional four or five party format in a few years. Was Mr. Glistrup and his Progress party not just a replay of Le Mouvement Poujade of the Fourth French Republic? Many convincing arguments could be made for the short lives of populist parties and populism was the label that was quite often put on the Prog-ress party. ... Predictions of a return to 'normalcy' were also made by political scientists. (Pedersen 1988: 272–273)

Similar thoughts prevailed among Norwegian politicians and political sci-entists concerning their Progress party's chance for long-term survival. The Danish party was first announced in 1972 and the Norwegian party one year later. Political scientists doubted the party would survive beyond the death of Anders Lange in the fall of 1974, and the other parties undoubtedly heaved a collective sigh of relief in 1977, when Progress failed to make the cut-off

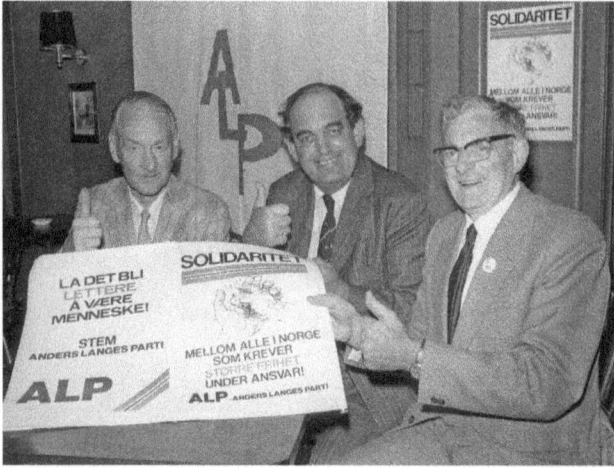

Figure 4.1 Mogens Glistrup and Ander Lange's Party leader Arve Lønnum (left) and its parliamentary leader Erik Gjems-Onstad at a press conference in Oslo on 31 August 1975. *Credit:* NTB Scanpix; *Photographer:* Erik Thorberg.

for Storting representation and lost all four of its seats. The Progress Party itself feared its days were numbered.[1] But the party was able to return to parliament in 1981 and has retained representation since, although with great fluctuations.

Even if the Progress parties had died in the 1990s, both would have out-lived the appropriateness of being considered 'flash' or even 'short-term' parties. Given the findings of Janda and Gillies's broadly comparative study of party stability, it would seem that the two Progress parties had already reached, by the early 1990s (the endpoint for our analysis of the institution-alisation process) an age where the 'average' party is more likely to survive than it is to disappear.

Survivability

But while persistence itself is one indicator of the potential for a party to persist longer, it is clearly not sufficient alone as evidence of institution-alisation, nor even of the one component we are calling 'durability'. For a party to be considered durable, it must also show ability to survive 'shocks'. Parties which have successfully survived name changes and/or organisational discontinuities (e.g. splits), for instance, have demonstrated this aspect of 'survivability'. For new parties founded by, and largely identified with, a particular 'charismatic' leader, substantial survival beyond the passing of that leader may also be a significant indicator of ability to survive severe shocks.

Similarly, a party identified initially with a particular issue could demonstrate survivability by withstanding attempts by other parties to 'steal' its issue.[2] Finally, a new potentially 'flash' party can demonstrate that it is a long-term survivor by coming back after an electoral disaster. By the early 1990s, each of the Progress parties had endured several of these types of shocks and had survived to tell about them.

Name Changes

While the Danish Progress Party (Fremskridtspartiet: Z[3]) had that name since its inception, its Norwegian counterpart began as 'Anders Lange's Party for a Strong Reduction in Taxes, Rates, and Public Intervention'. The name was changed to Progress Party (Fremskrittspartiet; acronym: FrP) in 1976, within two years of Lange's death. Though name changes may in some cases shake identification with a party, such does not seem to have been the case with this Norwegian party. Perhaps this is partly because the changes occurred so early in the party's existence, and partly because the new name was already familiar to Norwegian voters because of the success of the party's forerunner in Denmark. Regardless of the reason, this particular name change must itself be seen as a step towards institutionalisation by removing a personality's name from that of the party.

Organisational Discontinuities

Though neither of the Progress parties had been involved in a merger, both parties had by the early 1990s experienced splits and some other well-publicised resignations which certainly could be considered internal shocks of substantial magnitude.

In Norway:
In 1974, just a year after the founding of Lange's party, a charismatic young member by the name of Carl I. Hagen led a faction[4] that objected to the lack of routinised procedures, and especially the intentions of Lange to assume a 'super leader' status similar to that already accorded to Glistrup in Denmark. The dissenting faction split, and Hagen and others formed the splinter Reform Party. But soon after Lange's death later that same year, Hagen and his supporters returned to the fold. In 1978 Hagen was elected leader of the Progress Party, a position which he held until 2006.[5] No other party in post-war Norway has retained the same person as party leader for as long as two decades.

During Hagen's tenure as leader, the party endured many, often sharp, internal conflicts. From time to time, Hagen's leadership itself was either directly or indirectly responsible for the rifts. On some occasions, this was caused by positions or initiatives which Hagen took without consulting others in the organisation, for example in 1993, when Hagen departed dramatically from the party's traditional position on taxes without prior consultation with others in the party. Some of the conflicts were less national in scope, involving tensions between pro- and anti-Hagen groups in local or regional organisations, for example in the early 1990s, when the Bergen branch became so ridden with conflict that the national party organisation removed the local party secretary. Other conflicts arose over ideological differences, not surprisingly given that the party included both a 'pure liberalist' faction – a well-defined ideological faction favouring a minimalist state and opposing governmental regulation of immigration – and a more nationalistic conservative faction whose main concern was opposition to immigration.[6]

This ongoing situation of turmoil within the party was at times punctuated by resignations of public proportions. In 1992, for instance, an MP defected from the parliamentary group and in 1993 established the electorally unsuccessful 'The Unity Party – New Future'.[7]

In Denmark:
Already during its two first periods in the Danish parliament, tensions in the Progress Party's parliamentary group led to resignations of individual representatives; and in the party's own 'parliamentary diary' it was acknowledged that 'when we are not dealing with the party's three main political issues, opinions in the group are often strongly divided' (Folketingsgruppens dagbok 1976: 68). In 1978–79, close on the heels of Glistrup's conviction, a faction within the Danish party attempted to push it towards a more cooperative stance with regard to the other bourgeois parties, but Glistrup's more isolationist stance prevailed (McHale 1983: 173). The factionalism continued into the 1980s. Negotiations between the Progress Party and the four-party minority government that came into office following the 1981 election led to internal rivalries between Glistrup's 'hardliners' and the 'softies'. In the fall of 1983 four of the party's sixteen representatives left the party and yet another defected from the group in the spring of 1984 (Sauerberg 1988). No doubt these rivalries contributed to the party's poor performance in the elections of 1984.

Towards the end of the 1980s, the conflict between what were now called the 'Pianists' (after Pia Kjærsgaard, who entered parliament in 1984 and almost immediately became a leader among those seeking a more normal organisation and a more cooperative stance) and the Glistrup faction was brought to its apex. Glistrup defied the party whip and was denied renomination. Then, the party rules were adapted in 1991 and the 'Glistrup clause' – which had assured the founder a position on the main board for life – was removed (as described in more detail below).[8] Pia Kjærsgaard gained control of the party, while Glistrup made an unsuccessful attempt to launch a new party, Trivselspartiet (the Well-being Party).[9]

From their founding in the early 1970s through the early 1990s, both Progress parties persisted through factional disputes and public resignations, demonstrating a considerable ability to endure in spite of organisational disruptions. Both parties had survived important organisational discontinuities and had lived to fight another day. (More on the period since the early 1990s in chapter 8!)

Leadership Shocks

Anders Lange's party survived his death in 1974, and Mogens Glistrup's party endured throughout his eighteen months in prison (31 August 1983–11 March 1985). The ability of the parties to survive these losses of their founders (though, admittedly, that loss was only temporary in the Danish case) was especially significant because of how closely the parties were identified with the personalities of their original leaders.

The later ousting of Glistrup from the party he had founded can be seen as another leadership shock which the party survived. Though a number of organisational routines had been implemented and had solidified the position of Kjærsgaard by the time of Glistrup's ousting, he had continued to symbolise the party's original raison d'être.

Clearly, even prior to the 1990s both Progress parties had survived the shock of losing their original leader.[10]

Issue 'Stealing'

In elections following the breakthrough of the Progress parties, other parties (especially the Conservative parties) in both countries attempted to encroach upon the Progress parties' territory by speaking more forcefully than before for the curbing of taxes and against specific abuses of the welfare state (Harmel and Svåsand 1997). Yet, the Progress parties in both countries managed to maintain distinctive identities and electoral relevance partly because they were still perceived to be more genuinely committed to change, and partly by being the first to outspokenly address even newer issues such as the 'immigration problem'. In Norway, for example, 'immigration' became an issue in the 1987 local election campaign, promoted by the Progress Party. The Conservative Party, which lost more voters to the Progress Party than other parties, adopted a more restrictive view on immigration policy which it also pursued in government (Gudbrandsen 2010).

Electoral Disasters

Perhaps the most impressive evidence of a party's durability is its ability to survive dramatic electoral downturns. The Progress Party in Denmark had an extraordinary debut in 1973, becoming the second-largest party (winning 15.9 per cent of the vote and twenty-eight seats). Perhaps inevitably, decline set in, and by 1984 the party could manage just 3.6 per cent of the vote and only six seats (see Table 2.1a). In spite of recovery later, the party was not able to repeat its peak performance from the debut election.

The Norwegian party, which began with 5.0 per cent of the vote and four seats in 1973, lost all representation for the 1977–81 term, but then won four seats in 1981 (with 4.5 per cent of the vote) and two seats in 1985 (with 3.7 per cent of the vote). The 1989 elections were a great triumph for the party, going from two to twenty-two seats, again to be followed by a decline to ten seats in 1993.

Electoral volatility between elections is, of course, not unique to the Progress parties, but the loss of all seats – as the Norwegian party experienced in 1977 – certainly qualifies as an electoral shock. That party's ability to return to parliament in the next election is not just an indicator of survivability to outsiders, but must have been a confidence booster within the party as well.

Objective durability consists of records of both persistence and survivability. By the early 1990s both Progress parties had already attained sufficient age and survived enough 'shocks' to be considered at least moderately, if not highly, institutionalised on the dimension of durability. At the very least, it is clear that neither party could have any longer been considered simply a 'flash in the pan'.

INTERNAL INSTITUTIONALISATION

Routinisation

Both Progress parties were started by men intent on leading groups that would not be parties 'of the normal type'. In both cases the founder of the party opposed the idea of developing a party organisation on the same lines as other parties and in both cases organisational development quickly became a matter of internal dispute. In both, in spite of the founders' resistance, organisation eventually became formalised over time. In addition to the similarities, though, there were also some important differences in these two parties' development of organisation.

In Denmark

In his history of the early years of the Danish Progress Party, Larsen (1978) notes that at the first organisational meeting, Glistrup argued strongly against developing 'organisation' at either the national or the local levels, while others claiming to represent 'the grass roots' argued for the establishment of formal, local organisation. At the first full-fledged national convention in 1973, a compromise was reached whereby the national leadership would not organise the local level, but members could develop local associations if they wished to. Glistrup, while deploring the thought of spending a large quantity of his own time on organisational details, would still be available to provide 'leadership' at the national level.

In spite of Glistrup's original wishes, his party did develop a formal party organisation, though with some noteworthy differences from other Danish parties. Initially, the shape of that organisation was specifically intended to preserve Glistrup's influence as much as possible. Although provision was made for a national convention which would elect the party leadership, the composition of the convention was completely controlled by the central leadership itself and the convention was not empowered to decide anything regarding the party programme.[11] In fact, the agenda for the convention was to be set, and thereby could be limited, by the 'main board'. Thus, while granting the grass roots a forum for representation, the rules were tilted in favour of the main board and would therefore provide the leadership with considerable leeway concerning what should be discussed and by whom.

In practice as well as in the rules, power within the party was highly centralised, with the primary locus being the main board, and in reality Glistrup himself. According to the rules, both the political and organisational initiatives were the prerogatives of the main board, which solely decided on party policies and controlled party finances. The board was also given power to reject rules of local and provincial organisations, the guidelines for which were only vaguely formulated (Larsen 1978: 76). It could at any time change the rules for nominating candidates, and could at will interfere in the nominations of candidates in the individual constituencies. Though the rules initially provided that 'anyone who is invited by the main board, or represents the party in the Folketing, government, province or municipal council has the right to participate in the national convention' (Party rules, 1974, paragraph 5a), this provision was changed in 1976. Under the new rule, the board continued to exercise widespread influence over the composition of national conventions, for example, by appointing 80 delegates itself and further deciding how many delegates (with a minimum of 350) were to be chosen by local associations. The fact that the party was highly centralised is indisputable, but centralisation in itself is not inconsistent with internal institutionalisation. In fact, in a system such as Denmark's where state subsidies were, until 1987, given to the parliamentary group rather than the extra-parliamentary organisation, it was not unusual for power to be concentrated in the parliamentary group.

However, one rule – adopted in 1976 and pertaining to membership of the party's executive board – would remove any doubts about the 'abnormality' of this party's organisation. By the party's own rules, changes in party statutes could be made only by a two-thirds majority of the party conference. But in paving the way for adoption of the controversial 'Glistrup clause' the following year, the 1975 convention decided to allow the next convention to change rules by a simple majority. So in 1976, by a simple majority (and ulti- mately by acclamation; see Pedersen [1997: 54]), Mogens Glistrup was made a life member of its executive board. The Glistrup clause was, in other words, a very abnormal decision, arrived at by abnormal means. And it would prove to be, for many years to come, a major thorn in the side of members demand- ing *de*-personalisation and complete routinisation of the party's organisation.

One among the latter group would be Pia Kjærsgaard, co-leader of the party while Glistrup served his jail sentence, who would find removal of the clause to be much more difficult than its adoption had been. Though moder- ates (popularly known as the 'Pianists') had gained control of the party[12] dur- ing Glistrup's physical absence, his followers remained visible in parliament as well as among the grass roots. With Glistrup's re-entry into the Folketing group after the 1987 election, conflict between Glistrup's hardliners and Kjærsgaard's moderates again intensified.

At the 1989 national convention, the Pianists made their first attempt to remove the Glistrup clause. Kjærsgaard enjoyed a majority of delegate sup- port, but – with Glistrup's supporters now seeing the value in strict adherence to the two-thirds rule – fell eighteen votes short of that requirement,[13] with one pro-Glistrup delegate going so far as to proclaim his idol 'a gift from heaven' (*Information*, 25 September 1989).

But, at the 1991 convention, Glistrup was first denied renomination to parliament and then was officially expelled from the party he had founded.[14] And finally, the clause that had guaranteed his position of membership on the main board for life was rescinded as well, by a vote of 635 to 130 (Pedersen 1997: 211).[15]

While the founder's permanent seat on the main board was an important exception to complete routinisation of party organisation, in practice Glis- trup's role had already been reduced long before his clause was revoked. Glistrup's time in jail had given the other leaders an opportunity to prove their abilities to carry on in his absence. Kjærsgaard, the suppliant taking his seat when he was imprisoned in 1983, proved to be a competent leader in her own right, at the same time that Glistrup's star was being tarnished in the eyes of many of the party's members. The fact that Kjærsgaard, a moderate, was selected as parliamentary spokesperson in 1985 by 'routinised procedures' (over competitors), in spite of not being seen as a Glistrup 'insider', is itself an indicator of the extent to which the party had already moved in the direc- tion of a more 'normal' organisation.

Glistrup's removal stands as evidence that Progress had become fully rou- tinised (or very close to it) by the early 1990s. The removal of the Glistrup clause itself was a major step towards complete normalisation, given that the clause had undeniably been the single most glaring abnormality in the party's organisation.

As long as Glistrup had remained – both in person (or at least in spirit while in prison) and in his special position on the board – efforts to completely routinise the party would be stymied.[16] With his removal in 1991, the way was substantially cleared for the organisation to achieve more normal 'routinisation'.[17] Though Glistrup sympathisers would continue to challenge Kjærsgaard's leadership[18] and her attempts to move the party closer to the other parties of the 'right', those challengers would do so primarily by normal, routinised party procedures.

In Norway

While Glistrup's preference for a looser 'movement' approach seems to have been motivated at least in part by practical concerns regarding his own time restraints; Anders Lange was motivated genuinely and perhaps exclusively by a philosophical aversion to normal party organisation. Perceiving the existing parties as rigid, bureaucratic structures, immune to the demands and preferences of 'ordinary voters', Lange preferred instead 'spontaneous action'. 'Let us not do as the other parties do', Lange argued (Iversen 1998: 54), 'organise ourselves away from the issues and the voters'.

Virtually from the beginning, Carl I. Hagen – as informal party secretary – found himself at odds with the founder over organisational style. A lasting movement, in Hagen's view, would have to give supporters a feeling of participation and influence. And hence, regular party organisation would be necessary (Hagen 1984: 78ff). The rudimentary organisation created by Lange did formally assign to the national congress the prerogative to vote on the party's programme and general principles, and in that sense was somewhat more 'normal' than Glistrup's. Nevertheless, the organisational basis for the party was extremely weak, with only about 1020 members and around 50 local branches (Heidar and Svåsand 1994). For Hagen, the final straw came when Lange demanded the development of a 'super leader' position for himself similar to that which Glistrup had (already in fact, if not yet in the party rules) in Denmark.[19] Failing in his efforts to convince Lange that he should stand for the re-election that he most likely would win anyway, Hagen left Progress and joined the splinter Reform Party.

For the next few years, the Progress Party – lacking both the one-man organisation that was its founder and a set of 'normal', routinised procedures to effectively replace him – nearly disappeared in public opinion polls. But then in 1978, Hagen – who had returned after Lange's death, and whose personal commitment to developing normal organisation was beyond question – was selected as leader of the Progress Party. Not only would the party's organisation be changed dramatically; its fortunes would change as well.

Upon assuming his new post, Hagen enthusiastically oversaw the development of party organisation at all levels. The executive board was given 'the right to attend, speak and put forward proposals at the annual meeting of the province association' (FrP Rules[20] 1983). In 1986 this rule was extended to apply also at the local branch level. By 1990 the party had established local associations in more than half of the country's 448 municipalities (though several of those may have existed only on paper). The representational rules at the national level were also adapted in 1990 to fit those of the other non-socialist Norwegian parties.[21] But in other ways, Hagen's party developed special organisational features, including greater centralisation than was true for the other non-socialist parties.

The abnormal level of centralisation may itself, ironically, have resulted from the difficulties Hagen faced in trying to institutionalise a party whose supporters were generally opposed to rigid formalisation. In a revealing article in the party newspaper (*Fremskritt* 6 December 1991), Hagen was asked to explain what he meant when arguing for development of a strong 'organisational culture' within the party. Among his ten examples of good organisational culture was: 'When someone disagrees with you in a meeting you don't call him "an idiot" or "a fool", but say: "here there are different opinions", or "what you are saying may be right, but I see it this way!"' He warned party members and party representatives against placing themselves, their family, and their friends first when implementing party policy; consideration for the party had to come first. In spite of Hagen's culture-building efforts, though, media continued to report, on numerous instances, the complete breakdown of organisational routines in several local organisations. In 1991–92 in the city of Bergen, for instance, the national office found it necessary to intervene in local party affairs – to the extent of expelling members – when factional fighting broke out over control of the local organisation.

A dramatic success in the September 1989 national election brought new organisational challenges. Growth of the parliamentary group from two to twenty-two seats meant the possibility of fractionalisation and lack of control in the party organisation. At the outset, Hagen demonstrated a personal ability to keep the expanded group together, but at the national convention in the spring of 1990 he nevertheless proposed – and won acceptance for – modifying the party rules in an effort to routinise parliamentary coherence. The national executive committee and the national council were now given the final say in determining the political strategy for the parliamentary group, and were also made responsible for organising the group and controlling its budget. The committees also became the 'appeal boards' for minority views in the parliamentary group. The new rules in fact subordinated the parliamentary wing to the extra-parliamentary organisation, in sharp contrast to the other non-socialist parties. Under the new rules, the probability that Hagen could be out-manoeuvred by the parliamentary group was eliminated. While this may have amounted to routinisation *of* personalisation, it is still important to recognise that this itself had been accomplished through 'institutional design'.

Clearly, both of the Progress parties were more 'organised' by the early 1990s than they had been in infancy and than their original leaders had desired. Important differences existed, however, in how the parties had become fully routinised. The Norwegian party began with more specific stipulations regarding the role of the national congress, for instance, than was the case for the Danish party. And the Norwegian rules became even more elaborated through several iterations of changes spanning more than a decade. From the time Hagen assumed the reins of the Norwegian party in 1978, he had managed to increasingly routinise control in the hands of the organisational leader. From the time Dohrmann and Kjærsgaard took the reins in the Danish party in 1984, however, their efforts to further routinise Danish Progress were stymied by the continued organisational presence of the founder, and it was not until 1991 that his hold could be broken and the process significantly furthered.

Internal Value Infusion

For parties that began as personal projects of political entrepreneurs, infused with those entrepreneurs' own goals and ambitions, internal value infusion would involve the party becoming valued in its own right, aside from its founder and his/her original purposes and ambitions for the party. As noted above, empirical indicators of a party becoming 'valued for itself', by itself, would include development of a stable membership base and minimal defections of party representatives, even when leadership changes have occurred. And for parties whose founders were disdainful towards 'normal party organisation', routinisation itself could be seen as another indicator that the party had moved on from the founding purposes and ambitions. For both Progress parties, evidence supports the conclusion that internal value infusion had been achieved by or before the early 1990s.

In Denmark

According to Glistrup himself, his original motivation for starting the Progress Party came from the perception that the three-party bourgeois government of 1968–71 had not governed any differently from its socialist predecessors. Instead, it had 'shown a great lack of ability to create any new policies ... the result being an increase instead of a decrease in the evils they were elected to fight' (Glistrup 1978: 1). When the Conservative Party refused his request for nomination and showed no interest in his challenge to remain truer to its ideological dogma, Glistrup felt he 'had to found a new party and so I did'. While winning a seat for himself may have been on his mind as well, Glistrup recalled later that 'the main purpose of course was to preach a new political message'. This was to be a party with a distinctly anti-tax, anti-establishment message, but whose original purpose was as much or more so to influence the other parties (and particularly the Conservatives) as to become an institutionalised party itself.

Indeed, if institutionalisation were to mean becoming 'like the other parties' organisationally, Glistrup clearly would have shunned institutionhood. Glistrup's disdain for organisation 'of the normal type' might have been motivated in part by concerns over what it would mean for expenditure of his own time, but the disdain was nonetheless genuine. That the party would eventually routinise along lines which in many ways resembled other party organisations, and with programmes which themselves looked in some respects more 'normal' than Glistrup's original agenda, was hardly consistent with his original intentions for the party. Instead, it serves as evidence that the party was indeed capable of moving on from the founder and his designs.

That routinised procedures were used to expel Glistrup from his own party in 1991 is particularly noteworthy, since what happened afterward stands as further evidence of internal value infusion. Though Glistrup's expulsion could have resulted in significant defections of members and/or representatives from the party, these did not occur. By that time, the value of the party 'in its own right' had obviously overtaken the value previously attached to the founder alone.

Later events – including Glistrup's eventual return to the party – would challenge any notion that once achieved, value infusion cannot be reversed. More on that in chapter 8!

In Norway

Similar to Glistrup's intention in Denmark, Anders Lange's motivation for starting his namesake party was to scare other parties, even more so than to build up his own. The Conservative Party had recently been in government – but as in Denmark – the experience was less than gratifying for many grass-roots conservatives, who felt the party had abandoned its right-wing principles while governing. Getting the Conservatives' attention was Lange's primary mission.

Also similarly to Glistrup, Lange was far from an 'organisation man'. For Lange, the disdain for normal party organisation was based on principle, preferring spontaneous action to the rigid bureaucratic rules that were the stuff of the established parties. But with Lange's death and the eventual return of Hagen, the quintessential organisation man, the spontaneous action 'movement' gave way to more (though not completely) normal party organisation. The original purpose – to get another party's attention – also gave way to ambition for building a strong, lasting party with a difference – but in message more so than in structure.

The marked changes from the founder's design and purpose for his party brought no obvious tumult inside the party. Though the party's identity became as closely associated with Hagen as it had originally been with Lange, the transition also resulted – internally – in value for the party in its own right.

Ironically, this is perhaps best demonstrated by a tumultuous period caused by competing party values. By the early 1990s, the party had three identifiable factions: populists, value-oriented conservatives, and ideologically motivated liberalists (see Iversen 1998: 111). Though Hagen had nurtured the latter group in his own attempt to infuse additional value on the party, it proved to be the faction most difficult for him to handle. More will be said about this development in chapter 8. Suffice it for now to say that the value of 'party unity' superseded 'ideological purity', and some resignations resulted. The departure of the most outspoken liberalists was not the result of the party lacking value in its own right, however, but rather the consequence of the party having become infused with value on competing dimensions.

EXTERNAL INSTITUTIONALISATION

As Seen by the Electorate

How did voters view the Progress parties during the years covered by our analyses? Did they think of them as temporary protest vehicles, or as permanent fixtures, perhaps to be supported over the long term? To the extent that a party is perceived as temporary, it might seem 'safe' to vote for it once, simply to make a point. But the more permanent it is perceived to be, the more 'fixed' should be its own electorate, to the extent that it has one.

Lacking a direct indicator of the electorate's attitudes towards 'the Progress Party as "institution"', we must be satisfied in drawing inferences from various behavioural indicators. Perhaps the most obvious of those is the stability of the party's electorate over time, that is, the extent to which there is a core of voters who vote consistently for the party. A second indirect indicator is the proportion of the party's own electorate who decide 'early on' in an electoral campaign to vote for that particular party.[22]

Tables 4.1 and 4.1 consist of the percentages of the parties' voters in one election who voted for it again in the next election, as an indicator of the stability of the party's electorate over time. The data for the Danish Progress Party indicate that large percentages of its voters generally stayed with the party from one election until the next (though, admittedly, it is impossible to gauge from these data how many stayed with the party for more than two elections). Even when the party suffered its worst election, in 1984, it still maintained the support of nearly half of its 1981 electorate. The Norwegian data indicate that the Progress Party there did not experience the same level of continued support over most of its election cycles in the 1970s and 1980s. Only when the party had a triumphal election in 1989 did it maintain more than half of its voters from the previous election; when it suffered its greatest defeat in 1977, it maintained just 16.7 per cent of its 1973 voters. While it is true that we lack Danish data with which to do a direct comparison involving the maintenance of voters from the parties' first elections, it is also true that when the Norwegian party suffered its *second worst* election in 1985, it still maintained only 28.0 per cent of the voters from the previous election.

When a party's voters make up their minds to vote for the party is another indicator of 'electoral institutionalisation'. It is reasonable to assume that the more institutionalised a party, the earlier its electorate will decide to support it. As can be seen from table 4.2, the percentage of the Danish Progress Party's electorates making up their minds prior to the campaigns were consistently higher than for the Norwegian party, with the Danish percentages being generally high and even exceeding the average for the other Danish parties in four of the seven elections since 1975. Though the Norwegian Progress Party's voters were slower to decide than the average for the other Norwegian parties in each of the elections since 1973, the gaps were narrower in the later elections than in either 1973 (understandably, given that it was the party's debut election) or 1981. Though it is true that the closing of the gap was due in part to the rest of the parties' electorates taking longer to decide, it is still the case that the percentages of Norwegian Progress voters deciding early increased appreciably after the first two elections for which we have data. Indeed, the voters for Danish Progress

Table 4.1   Percentage of Progress Party Voters Repeating their Vote from One Election to the Next

a. Denmark	%	b. Norway	%
1979–81	72.0	1973–77	16.7
1981–84	47.5	1977–81	47.4
1984–87	87.1	1981–85	28.0
1987–88	89.0	1985–89	63.0
1988–90	68.8	1989–93	24.1

Table 4.2   Timing of the Electorate's Decision to Vote for the Progress Parties Versus Total Electorate (Per cent)

		Before Campaign (%)	During Campaign (%)	Last Days (%)	N
a. Norway					
1973	FrP	25.0	40.6	34.4	32
	Total	76.6	10.1	12.7	
1981	FrP	30.5	40.7	28.8	59
	Total	72.6	8.9	10.7	
1985	FrP	57.6	25.8	16.7	66
	Total	77.1	8.6	12.1	
1989	FrP	56.8	16.5	26.2	206
	Total	58.3	18.2	23.3	
1993	FrP	45.1	14.6	40.2	82
	Total	57.1	16.5	25.5	
b. Denmark					
1975[i]	FrP	64.9	14.6	20.5	151
	Total	73.6	11.9	13.5	
1977	FrP	80.4	11.6	8.0	112
	Total	72.7	11.5	15.5	
1979	FrP	78.4	8.1	13.5	111
	Total	76.6	10.1	13.0	
1984	FrP	56.8	16.5	26.2	206
	Total	58.3	18.2	23.3	
1987	FrP	80.4	11.6	8.0	112
	Total	72.7	11.5	15.5	
1988	FrP	78.4	8.1	13.5	111
	Total	76.6	10.1	13.0	
1990	FrP	71.4	20.0	8.6	35
	Total	79.0	11.5	9.5	

Sources: Norway: Norwegian Election Analysis Program; Denmark: Danish Election Surveys. (Data provided by the Norwegian Social Science Data Services (NSD). NSD bears no responsibility for the selection of or interpretation of the data.)
[i]This question was not asked in the 1973 election survey in Denmark.

generally decided as early as the voters for the other Danish parties, and the voters for Norwegian Progress became comparable to Norway's other parties' electorates as well.

Both in terms of its percentage of repeat voters and its percentage of early deciders, the Danish Progress Party appears to have been more institutionalised in the electorate than its Norwegian counterpart. And from both indicators, it appears that the Danish party established an 'attached electorate' early in its existence, certainly earlier than the Norwegian party. But while the Danish party's electorate may have become established earlier and at a higher level, it seems reasonable to conclude that by the early 1990s both parties had achieved institutionalisation within the electorate, especially as compared to other parties in their own systems.

As Seen by Other Parties

From the standpoint of other parties in the system, external institutionalisation refers to the extent to which a 'new' party is taken seriously by at least some of the other parties as a new actor that must be reckoned with over the long haul, rather than simply ignored as a passing fancy. In this regard, a party's level of institutionalisation is gauged in the eye of the beholding party, and need not have much to do with actual, internal routinisation. Nor is it necessary that the party in question be 'liked' by the rest; it must only be seen by them as an actor that must be taken into account when making plans for the future.

Parties reveal their attitudes towards the institutionalisation of other parties both in their public pronouncements and in their actual behaviour. In the early years of the two Progress parties, statements of other parties' leaders were often designed to maximise distance between themselves and Progress. In part this reflected the established parties' reactions to Progress's unorthodox positions on regulation and public spending (and later on immigration) and to their early, unorthodox political style (including Glistrup's declaration on television in 1971 that tax evaders were heroes to be equated with the resistance movement, and Lange's appearance at a party leaders' televised debate wearing a toy replica of an old Viking sword and drinking egg liqueur). And in part, it resulted from the attitudes of the Progress parties towards others; both made concerted efforts to promote themselves as something 'new and different', waging battle against the *'gammelpartiene'* (old-time parties) that allegedly ignored the wishes of voters. The immediate reaction of the other parties, both in Denmark and in Norway, was to have nothing to do with the newcomers.

> All 28 of us were debutants and we were met with the most icy coldness imaginable...

> They simply hated us – and they still do. (Glistrup 1978: 4)

> We were met with a front of ice in the Storting. (Slettebø, in interview with *Bergens Tidende*, 27 January 1983)

The general public approach of the established parties was to treat the new right-wing counterparts with a mixture of disdain and public disregard. For the Conservative parties, in particular, any flirtation with Progress could have jeopardised other non-socialist coalition alternatives. And when the support for the Progress Party in Norway dropped to below the representation threshold in 1977 and nosedived for the Danish party in 1984, the leaders of the other parties undoubtedly felt the public disdain-and-disregard approach had been a wise choice. At those times, few political commentators expected that the Progress parties would be able to make a comeback.

But come back they did. In the Norwegian case, the party mustered 13 per cent of the votes in the 11 September 1989 Storting elections, giving the party 22 of the 165 seats. In Denmark the party increased its representation from six to nine seats in 1987 and further to sixteen seats in 1988. Concurrently, there was a notable, though not yet complete, change in the attitude and behaviour of other parties towards the Progress parties. This thawing of the ice-front with which the parties were first met took three forms, though to different degrees, in the two countries.

First, statements (at least from some parties, especially the Conservatives) with regard to the Progress parties, while still often designed to emphasise serious differences in both viewpoints and style, were generally less vitriolic than earlier (Glasser 1994: 94–101). The Progress parties were no longer dismissed by the others as 'a bunch of village nuts', a characterisation which was now thought to have backfired against the 'old-time parties' accused of ignoring ordinary voters (a sizable minority of whom had now voted for Progress at least once). Perhaps most telling in the Norwegian case was a public statement by the leader of the Socialist Left Party in 1988: 'We need to take Carl I. Hagen as a politician seriously. We need to discuss with him, become as bold as him, and admit that he discusses issues that are important to people'.[23]

Second, recognising the Progress parties to be a more substantial and long-term threat than previously thought, other parties adjusted their own programmes accordingly. Lower taxation, deregulation, privatisation, and more restrictive immigration policy now made their way into the platforms of the more established parties[24] (see Strøm and Leipart 1989).

And third, the Conservative parties – first in Denmark but eventually in Norway as well – would now find the Progress parties to be at least sufficiently respectable to warrant entering negotiations with them for their potential governmental support. This tendency was first noticeable, and had gone the furthest by the early 1990s, in the Danish case. Following the Danish election of 1981, the new four-party non-socialist minority government negotiated with the Progress Party for parliamentary support, and later governments did the same (Petersen and Svensson 1989: 23–25). In 1989, for the first time, the governing parties formally negotiated an agreement with Progress for its support of the budget bill. And in advance of the 1994 election, the 100-point programme devised by Kjærsgaard as a possible basis for governing was actually given serious consideration by leaders of other parties.[25] There can be no doubt that by this time the Progress Party was clearly seen as having governmental relevance at the national level.

The picture is a bit more fuzzy in Norway. In two electoral periods, 1985–89 and 1989–93, the Progress Party held the balance in the Storting between the Socialist parties (Labour and Socialist Left) and the traditional non-socialist parties (the Conservatives, the Centre Party, the Liberals, and the Christians). The differences in policy profiles between the Progress party, on the one hand, and the Christian People's Party and the Centre Party on the other, prohibited the building of a majority-based, non-socialist government in either period. In spite of Progress's earlier cooperation on the non-Socialist minority government's 1986 budget bill, that government chose to disregard Progress's ultimatum regarding tax increases.[26] That the government would ignore Progress's wishes (and threat) to its own peril was demonstrated in March 1986 when the Progress Party refused to support a petrol tariff increase, thereby causing the government to fail on a vote of confidence. The next non-socialist government (1989–90) would again formally negotiate for the Progress Party's thirteen votes for the budget bill. Still, there was no indication that Progress would be invited to sit at the government table any time soon.

But while the Danish party may have seemed a bit closer to government participation by the early 1990s, it is clear that both of the Progress parties had achieved institutionalisation in the eyes of other parties. Scorned in the beginning, and then ignored, neither party could be so easily dismissed in future strategic considerations.

CONCLUSION

Application of our three-pronged conceptual framework to the Progress parties reveals not only why it is important to treat the components separately, but also that the two Progress parties had become fully institutionalised by the early 1990s, defying the negative, earlier predictions of well-informed observers. If there were still differences between the two parties with regard to institutionalisation, those differences would have had to do with *how* the parties had become institutionalised, and with *what* had been institutionalised in each case, rather than with the degree of institutionalisation (more on these topics in later chapters!). Indeed, even if either party were to have died in later years, it would be accurate to consider it the death of an 'institutionalised' party. It follows, then, that it is legitimate to ask why the predictions were wrong in the first place. We shall do that over the next three chapters.

NOTES

1. Carl I. Hagen in an interview with *Verdens Gang,* 13 September 1977.
2. For a study of how established parties sometimes appropriate the issues of niche parties, see Meguid (2001).

3. There had already been another attempt to register a party by the name of Progress Party (Fremskridtspartiet). Glistrup acquired both the right to use that name and the collected signatures for just 800 Danish kroner. 'Z' was the letter assigned to the Progress Party on Danish ballot papers. 'Z' was selected by Glistrup to symbolise that the Progress Party was radically different from the established parties. Such letters are frequently used in the media as abbreviations for the party names and are also used by the parties themselves. Thus, the Progress Party usually displayed a large 'Z' on the cover of election programmes and party documents.

4. In this book we are taking some liberty in the use of the word 'faction'. Though we have in some other places (e.g. Harmel and Tan 1996) distinguished between 'faction' and 'tendency' on the basis that factions are formally organised and tendencies are not, here we use the term faction to encompass both organised factions and looser tendencies.

5. More on this in chapter 8.

6. For more information on the three factions of the Progress Party at the time, including the liberalists and the conservatives, see Iversen (1998: 111).

7. In 1994 the liberalistic wing of the party – with its own stronghold in the party's youth movement – split away and formed the 'Free Democrats' political organisation. More on this in chapter 8.

8. An earlier attempt to do this in 1989 had failed.

9. Kjærsgaard's attempt to push the party towards the political centre in Denmark was halted on 25 September 1995, when the hardliners in the parliamentary group defeated her candidates for party leadership positions. In the organisational turmoil that followed, Kjærsgaard defected from the party on 6 October, together with three other MPs, and launched Dansk Folkeparti (Danish People's Party). More on these events in chapter 8, where we consider them to be part of the process of 'de-institutionalisation' of the party.

10. Whether the Danish party could survive the further shock of losing Kjærsgaard as leader in 1995 is part of the story of 'de-institutionalisation' to be told in chapter 8.

11. For details, see Bille 1992.

12. Though begun earlier, this process was effectively completed at the party's national convention in 1987, just in advance of Glistrup's return to the parliamentary group. See Bille (1997: 107), for a chronicle of the relevant events of the 1987 convention.

13. Reminiscing over what had contributed to his decline within the party, Glistrup said: 'The day I accepted the need for a regular party organisation, I lost' (*Information* 17/18 November 1990).

14. As demonstration of how abnormal the Glistrup clause was known to be, even internationally, it is worth noting that the Norwegian party had no formal contact with the Danish party while Glistrup was in charge. Hagen declined to have anything to do with his Danish counterpart because the party was 'undemocratic', due to the Glistrup clause. When the Glistrup clause was removed by the Danish party in 1991, the two Progress parties established a formal linkage in the form of a cooperation committee. See Heidar and Svåsand (1997).

15. There was a separate vote on excluding him from the party: 603 yes, 166 no.

16. In fact, according to Bille (1997: 303–304, 320), there were almost no changes in formal party rules between 1976 and 1991.

17. As if to demonstrate that fact, the 1991 convention itself went further and effectively reduced the main board's control over the composition of future conventions. No longer could the board designate 80 delegates by itself; the maximum number of delegates from local branches would now increase from 350 to 1500; and all of those delegates would now be distributed according to size of membership and size of support for the party at the previous election rather than by the more flexible rules of the past.

18. It was by application of 'normal procedures' that Kjærsgaard was denied the right to simultaneously hold both parliamentary and extra-parliamentary offices. In 1994, when Kjærsgaard announced that she would run for extra-parliamentary chair of the party while remaining as parliamentary spokesperson, she was rebuffed. If the party had gone along with her wishes, it would have been breaking with the party's tradition (though there was no written rule to this effect) of not allowing the same person to serve simultaneously in both parliamentary and extra-parliamentary offices (see Bille 1997: 107).

19. According to Iversen, Lange had also 'made it clear that he would not take part in forming a party unless it included his name and he became chair' (1998: 18). Lange did not succeed in getting his special position written into the party rules.

20. Translated from the Norwegian title: *Fremskrittspartiet Vedtekter*.

21. A distinction between socialist and non-socialist party organisations was the ex officio representation of MPs in party organs in the latter group of parties.

22. A third potential indicator, for which data are not available for our cases for our time period, would consist of the extent to which the voters actually agree with the party's message.

23. Erik Solheim, chair of the Socialist Left Party, quoted in Hagen (2007: 153).

24. Though the Conservative parties in both countries did – in the Norwegian case almost immediately and in the Danish case eventually – alter some of their own policy positions in the Progress parties' directions earlier than the late 1980s (see Harmel and Svåsand 1997), as time went on, more parties and more issues became involved.

25. As it turned out, though, the election results made such a government an impossibility.

26. For more on this agreement, see Hagen 2007: 102–104.

Chapter 5

Institutionalisation

'Impediments' and the Progress Parties

'At the time of its rise, most political observers were inclined to dismiss the party as an ephemeral, unimportant, and somewhat comical phenomenon, although a few expressed their fear that it posed a threat to democracy. ... No one then thought that the party would endure for very long, or that it would have much impact on the policy making process'. When Michael Stein (1973: 3) wrote these words, he was describing early perceptions of the Ralliement des Credistes, Quebec's wing of Canada's Social Credit Party. But precisely the same words give an accurate account of early reactions to the two Progress parties. As we have already noted, predictions of early demise with little consequence were not limited to politicos in the two countries, but were proffered by political scientists as well. And their predictions were not without theoretical support from relevant literature. Though it has at times been presumed that entrepreneurial right-wing protest parties would be unable to endure and ultimately institutionalise (see, for example, Bolleyer 2013: Ch. 7; DeClair 1999: 59; Sartori 1975: 133), it is more common to find statements limited to the tremendous difficulties and hence unlikelihood of such parties doing so. After all, institutionalisation is thought to be difficult for new parties of movement origins (e.g. see DeClair 1999: 77; Frankland 1995; Hirsch 1998: 189; Offe 1998: 173), or with charismatic leadership (e.g. see Green and Binning 1997: 102; Panebianco 1988: 147), or based in 'protest' (e.g. Sankiaho 1971: 42–44; Williams 1972: 160). Entrepreneurial right-wing protest parties commonly begin with all three.

Our purpose in this chapter is not to 'test' the assumptions of non-institutionalisability of the Progress parties; those assumptions have already been overturned in chapter 4. Instead, our purpose here and in the next two chapters is to carefully examine the experiences of the Progress parties with regard to each of the factors mentioned above – origins, message, and especially leadership – with an eye towards identifying any 'special' conditions that may have made it possible for *these* parties to institutionalise, in spite of the presumed odds against them. Because in an entrepreneurial party the message and the organisational style are products of the founding leader, even more so than in other new parties, the bulk of this chapter and the next two will be devoted to developing and applying theory on the relationship of leadership skills and orientations to the institutionalisation of such parties.

Panebianco (1988: 161), after carefully explaining why it is so difficult for charismatic parties to institutionalise but still recognising that there have been rare cases of success, laid out a challenge for future studies to 'isolate the conditions which allow charismatic parties to institutionalise'. In this chapter, we take up that challenge for the class of parties we have labelled 'right-wing protest parties of entrepreneurial origins', with a brief discussion of extant theory and its application to the Progress parties. Then in chapter 6, we proceed to more elaborate development of theory on the role of leadership (and particularly leadership change) in the institutionalisation of right-wing parties with entrepreneurial origins, and finally in chapter 7 consider the experiences of the Progress parties in the light of the latter theoretical framework.

MOVEMENT ORIGINS

Much of what has been written about the difficulties in institutionalising right-wing protest parties has focused upon schisms that 'inevitably' develop between those wishing to hold on to the movement origins and those who wish to engineer a transition to a full-fledged party. Prominent among this literature is Stein's (1973) treatment of the development of the Ralliement Creditistes in Quebec.

While acknowledging that tendencies to factionalism may be present in other protest movements as well, Stein argues that these tendencies 'are likely to be particularly acute in right-wing protest movements' because of the simultaneous occurrence of two factors. First, the nature of the right-wing appeal is such that it is likely to be difficult to expand the movement, with resulting frustrations (more on the 'narrow appeal' shortly!). And second,

> if the movement is reformist rather than revolutionary, as protest movements by definition are, then the set of ideas around which the leaders rally is likely to be loosely defined and subject to a considerable range of different interpretations. These two factors will contribute simultaneously to the emergence within the core group of activists of opposition groups which will challenge the prevailing leaders. (18)

Indeed, though Stein himself does not explicitly say so, it seems implicit that the more ad hoc nature of right-wing ideology itself, compared to left-wing, creates more 'room to play' on both issue positions and strategy and tactics, and hence more room for serious schisms as well. And while the resulting factionalism may be a continuing situation, it could be most pronounced during a couple of transition periods which Stein discusses at some length.

Starting with a model of 'three broad phases in a movement's development', each of which is associated with a different strategy and type ('generation') of leader, Stein argues that there is potential for a major schism each time one phase (and its leader(s)) is challenged by the next. The first phase (mobilisation) is led by 'prophets or men of words' who are well qualified to rally support behind the movement's central ideas. The second phase (consolidation) is led by 'administrators or agitators' skilled in organising the movement into specialised units as the group's energies are 'directed away from recruitment and towards the achievement of concrete results'. Finally, in the third phase (stabilisation), 'statesmen or pragmatic politicians' use their skills to steer the movement towards becoming either a conventional party (or interest group) or 'an educational and ideological adjunct to the political power holders in society'. During each new phase, a new generation and its strategies are pitted against the old, with the resulting schism possibly threatening the continued existence of the movement. Hence, the notion that factionalism associated with right-wing protest movements becomes acute on the road to institutionhood, making it unlikely that they will reach the destination!

In examining whether, or to what extent, the Progress parties fit the model of factionalism in parties that begin as movements, it is necessary first to consider the extent to which these parties actually did begin as movements. Certainly, the original leaders both thought of their parties as being other than ordinary organisationally, and both of them wanted it that way, though for somewhat different reasons. (Lange was philosophically opposed to normal organisation, while Glistrup's opposition was at least partly motivated by concern over losing control, as well as concern for his own time.) But saying that the founders opposed normal party organisation is not to say that the parties began as *established* social movements of the type Stein is describing.

Unlike Stein's own case of the Social Credit Party in Quebec, where the party was an outgrowth of a movement that had existed for forty-seven years before the party's birth, the Danish Progress Party's historical roots were very short. Mogens Glistrup entered the public eye for the first time with his television appearance in January 1971. The gathering of his friends in Tivoli Gardens, where he announced his intention to form the party, took place on 22 August 1972. The party was officially registered in July 1973 and produced its first electoral surprise five months later. From the television debut to the first election was just three years.

So, while Glistrup personally preferred a loose, 'movement' style of non-organisation, and though the first electoral success was clearly due to something other than organisational effort, it would be wrong to conclude that the Progress *Party* was an outgrowth of an established Progress *movement*. The issue of whether to have a 'normal' party organisation was joined at its very first meeting, not several years after the group was formed. And by 1973, Glistrup had already yielded to the demands for local organisation. Disputes over strategy (including further organisational development) were to continue for several years and would be the cause of several notable resignations, and eventually would lead to the expelling of the party founder. In this case, a number of factors may have contributed to the tempering of schismatic behaviour:

1. Glistrup was not so much philosophically as practically opposed to party-style organisation, thus perhaps making it a bit easier for him to compromise with those wanting normal organisation at the local level.
2. It was clear almost from the beginning that a *party* was being formed, and hence there would be no large 'founding' group wedded to the movement style. Relatedly, the decision to allow development of normal party structures was made early enough so that it did not require displacement of one 'generation' by another.
3. Glistrup's year and a half in prison in 1983–85 gave the more organisation-prone sub-leaders a freer hand to structure the party according to their wishes.
4. All of the other factors were operating in a context where 'ordinary' party organisation does not require very much extra-parliamentary organisation in the first place. In the Danish context, parties tend to operate from their parliamentary headquarters, and so it was for the Progress Party.

These factors probably contributed to the smoother ride (though certainly not without bumps) of Glistrup's party compared to the experiences of parties growing out of long-established movements such as Quebec's Social Credit Party and Germany's Greens. In fact, the Danish party's early years were also somewhat less schismatic than for its Norwegian counterpart.

Just as Lange's own hatred of organisation ran deeper than Glistrup's, it can be argued that the 'movement roots' of the Norwegian party were a bit longer and broader than was the case for the Danish party. Whereas Glistrup first 'awoke' the Danish public with his television appearance in January 1971 and launched his party at the restaurant press conference in August 1972, Lange's newsletter had been offering wake-up calls in Norway since the 1950s (Iversen 1998: 14–15), at least fifteen years prior to the initial party meeting in the Oslo theatre.

Some who were enlisted into Lange's 'army' that night certainly thought they were joining a party, and expected it to look and act like one. We have already noted that young Carl I. Hagen was among them. What Hagen lacked in years was made up for in self-confidence. The generational schism over strategy would not take years to develop in Lange's party; in just over one year Hagen had argued with Lange over the organisational approach and had lost, leaving then and shortly thereafter joining the splinter Reform Party.[1] Under normal political circumstances this might well have marked the beginning of the end for Lange's party, but an abnormal circumstance interceded: Lange died.

Hagen's return to the party in May 1975 presaged a new direction for the party organisationally; his selection as leader in 1978 assured it. Hagen's party, unlike Lange's, would be a party organised along 'normal' party lines.

Under Hagen's leadership the party made efforts to organise at the local and provincial levels. In 1975 the party was able to nominate candidates for the local elections in only 12 per cent of the municipalities, but in 1987 more than a third of the municipalities had Progress candidates, and in 1995, 193 of a total of 435 municipalities had Progress candidates. Hagen, in fact, would not hesitate to point to the importance of strong organisation in the success of socialist and labour parties as an argument for his party's new emphasis on organisation (from transcript of Harmel's interview with Hagen, 1988). The idea of Progress as a movement became, under Hagen, little more than historical artifact.

So the Norwegian party, more so than its Danish counterpart, fit the model of schismatic behaviour taking the form of major splits over organisational strategy in parties formed from 'movements', and indeed it did suffer a significant split over the issue.[2] But the schism occurred and was resolved at an earlier stage than has often been the case for such parties. Lange's death so early in the party's development and the availability of alternative, organisation-prone leadership to eventually replace him may have contributed to Progress being an 'exception to the rule'.

In both the Norwegian and the Danish cases, in fact, special circumstances related to leadership (and especially leadership change) go far in explaining how the parties avoided fatal schisms; although in Denmark the leadership factors operated in a context where such schisms would be less likely in the first place. After a brief discussion of the difficulties in institutionalising right-wing protest parties' messages, we will have much more to say on the special role of leadership factors in not only normalising organisation, but in institutionalising generally.

THE MESSAGE

It is part of the 'common knowledge' concerning right-wing protest parties that they lack a *positive*, unifying ideology to sustain their supporters in

electoral downtimes. The very label of 'protest' signifies being *against* something; the common assumption is that such parties, especially if they are on
the right of the political spectrum, are not *for* anything in particular. Opposed
to something or everything, they lack a broad, coherent plan for doing things
differently.

Such protest parties may initially act as a vehicle to attract protesters of all
types, according to the argument, but they will fall into disfavour once the
electorate learns just how simple-minded they really are. After a few electoral
failures, even the supposed diehards will take their protest elsewhere. But this
argument ignores two important facts. First, parties that begin as just protest
vehicles may, given certain conditions, become more moderate and reformist over time. And second, there is nothing inherently 'uninstitutionalisable'
about the right-wing message, as evidenced by many highly institutionalised
right-wing parties in existence today. Both of these correctives are relevant
to the experiences of the Progress parties.

It is clear that both parties were, or at least were generally perceived to be,
merely parties of protest when they began. That is, it was very clear what they
opposed, but if they were *for* anything, it was apparently just the flip side of
what they were against. In Denmark, it is true that Glistrup himself developed
a multi-point programme which went beyond just statements of opposition.[3]
However, he began that programme with just the three broad points – opposition to income tax, red tape bureaucracy, and the jungle of laws and regulations – and then boldly stated that 'on all other points the Progress Party
leaves its supporters free' (Glistrup 1978: 7). And not only did the party run
in its early elections on only those three issues, but Glistrup himself was
quoted in the press as rejecting the need for a more general programme: 'All
other purposes are outside of the Progress Party's concern' (*Morgenposten*,
18 March 1973, as quoted in Damborg and Østerby [1973: 50]), certainly
justifying the general impression that Progress was about just three points of
protest. In Norway, Lange's party conducted its first campaign on a platform
consisting of one sheet of paper, with one side listing ten statements starting
with 'We are tired of ...', and the other side listing ten statements beginning
with 'What we are for ...'. In their earliest years, both parties could be accu-
rately described as simply 'right-wing protests'.

In systems where other far-right-wing parties were already identified with
similar positions, or even earlier in Norway and Denmark when questioning fundamental aspects of the welfare state would have fallen completely
on deaf ears, both parties might have been relegated to permanent footnote
status as 'short-term protest phenomena'. But in Denmark and Norway in
the 1970s and 1980s, the parties seemed to hit a responsive chord within the
electorate. These parties questioned some of the fundamental values underlying the countries' prevailing social democratic ideologies at a time when a

significant portion of the population were themselves questioning some of those values.

The Progress parties did not die in their early years due to lack of a positive message, but instead survived to experience a number of electoral successes. Though the electoral successes may be explained in part by simple protest, and especially in the beginning by general turmoil in the party systems; it is also plausible – especially in the later years – to attribute some of the support to more basic changes in societal values, especially (but not necessarily only) among the younger generations. According to Einhorn and Logue's analysis in 1988 of party system change in Scandinavia,

> For the older generation which had known poverty and periodic unemployment, the benefits of the welfare state were worth any cost in bureaucratisation. But for the younger generation which had grown up with full employment and relative affluence, the mechanism that made the welfare state work became the target for protest. (1988: 180–181)

According to their argument, the 'protest' was linked to changes in deep-seated values:

> There is a great deal of evidence that the solidaristic values or reciprocal obligation and responsibility were generation specific. ... A growing egotism seems to be taking their place. There is evidence of a marked generational shift in utilisation of welfare state benefits that has increased take-up rates (and costs) without any appreciable improvement in welfare. ... The political expression of this egotism has focused on taxes. (1988: 173)

If in fact the Progress parties' votes, or at least a significant number of them, were reflecting protest based not just on circumstances of the moment but rather on fundamental value change, this would presumably indicate potential for the parties to establish long-term support by offering policy alternatives that conformed to the 'new' values. And it should have been easier for the new parties than for the old ones, all of which had become associated in voters' minds with the status quo, to take advantage of the new circumstances. By this line of reasoning, the Progress parties would have been well positioned to become more than just protest vehicles. Their unique placement on the far right of their countries' political spectra, rather than being a hindrance, would actually have given these new parties a special advantage in their particular contexts.

If the enhanced hindrance to institutionalisation that is alleged for a 'right-wing' protest message, in particular, stems from assuming that message to be 'conservative', 'authoritarian', and 'reactionary' – unlike the 'new' values associated with parties of the left – then it is easier to see why the Progress parties' messages were less of a hindrance to them in the setting within which they developed. Unlike some of their peers in other countries such as the Republikaner (a racist reaction to increased immigration) and the Deutsche Volksunion in Germany or the National Front and the British National Party in Great Britain – parties for whom those more traditional descriptors would apply – the Progress parties did not begin as authoritarian, anti-immigration vehicles. Rather, they began as anti-tax, anti-big government, quasi-libertarian parties which saw in their positions what their names would seemingly imply – progress, not regress. For both parties, the addition of the anti-immigration positions to their profiles came later, during the mid-1980s, and even then with the emphasis on the economic dimension (see Andersen and Bjørklund 1990: 211–212). Both parties saw themselves as offering, albeit with rather minimalist platforms, images of a new, better, and different future for themselves and many of their fellow Danes and Norwegians. It is our contention that this – coupled with societal changes resulting in a receptive clientele – is in fact an important part of the explanation for the Progress parties' successes in the period of our study.[4]

But had it not been for an internal factor – leaders willing and able to broaden the programme – the Progress parties might well have lost their positional advantage. The societal change was instrumental in creating the opportunity to connect with a substantial block of voters in a 'positive' way, but the message would now have to be reshaped (or at least broadened) in order to do so. Had the parties failed to expand beyond their original narrow and negative appeals, their early electoral downturns might well have been permanent. Their 'natural constituencies', to the extent that they existed, might well have gone to other parties, possibly including even newer parties. But under the more moderate leadership of Kjærsgaard and Hagen, the Progress parties significantly expanded their message. What had been 'a few simple points' now grew into detailed and wide-ranging programmes.[5] As of 1989, the Danish party's platform was housed in a neatly printed document of thirty pages, covering all aspects of society. Even more importantly, as part of the strategy for seeking acceptance among other non-socialist parties, the Danish Progress Party went to great length to distance itself from its own recent past. The 100-point programme launched before the 1994 election explicitly highlighted the moderation of the party: 'We are not an all-or-nothing party. As other parties we stand for our program. But we are willing to go far to have an impact' (Pia Kjærsgaard, in the introduction to the 100-point programme). A similar expansion had taken place in the Norwegian party's platform. By 1989, what had begun as the single sheet of paper had grown to a booklet of ninety pages, complete with a four-page index covering everything from Norwegian participation in the UN to deregulation of the reindeer business.

While both parties continued to oppose many aspects of the status quo, it was also easier now to see some of the things the parties were *for*. They continued to oppose abuses and expansion of the welfare state (though neither party ever opposed the welfare state concept in general; see Strøm and Leijphart 1989: 271); regulation of 'normal' citizens (i.e. non-criminals); big bureaucracy; certain subsidies (including agriculture in Norway and the arts in Denmark); government-sponsored foreign aid; and of course, taxes. But they also *favoured* not only less of all of the above, but also more free enterprise; provision for private hospitals and health care; private sector responsibility for correcting environmental problems; individual freedoms; and direct democracy through more use of referenda. In addition, in Norway the Progress Party was the *only* party to offer ideas for restructuring political decision-making, including abolition of the provincial councils and transfer of more power to the local level. The content of the platforms had clearly become at least as much 'reformist' as it was 'protest'.

As with the development of more normal organisational styles, the broadening of the parties' messages can be attributed in part to the timely transitions to 'second-generation' leadership. Both Glistrup and Lange were on record as favouring the original, narrow, hardline approach. But Glistrup's imprisonment and Lange's death brought to the fore new leaders who were as (or more) interested in governing as preaching. That these transitions could take place successfully was itself somewhat remarkable, however, given the strong attachment of the parties (or at least their identities) to their founders. That is a third alleged obstacle in the way of institutionalising right-wing protest parties, and we turn to it now.

CHARISMATIC LEADERSHIP

Protest parties which lack a unifying 'ideology' in their early years have often found a replacement in a strong, unifying leader (see Taggart 1996: 36–37). Hence, it is not uncommon for right-wing protest parties to be 'charismatic' (or 'personalistic', or in our own terminology 'entrepreneurial') parties as well. According to Panebianco, the leader of such a party

> founds the party, proposes its ideological goals, and selects its social bases by himself. He becomes – in the activists' and external supporters' eyes – the only interpreter and living symbol of the 'doctrine', as well as the only means to its future realisation. A total overlap of the leader's image and party identity is the *sine qua non* of charismatic power. (1988: 145)

Though neither Lange nor Glistrup were personally 'charismatic' in the more general sense of that word, their infant parties certainly did fit Panebianco's description of charismatic parties.

The fact that the two Progress parties had charismatic origins gave observers an additional reason to doubt their abilities to institutionalise. As Panebianco has summarised the common knowledge concerning the problems such parties face:

> Institutionalisation is not ... very likely in a charismatic party. The leader often deliberately tries to block the process; the charisma cannot be objectified, and the organisation is forced to fold at its leader's political eclipse. (1988: 147)

In those exceptional charismatic parties which have institutionalised, the process has presumably been far from simple, involving 'an objectification or routinisation of charisma, a transfer of loyalties from the leader to the organisation, and a growing divergence between the party's organisational identity and the leader's personal political fortune' (1988: 147).

Given that both Progress parties began as 'charismatic' by Panebianco's definition, and that both survived the absence of their original leaders and became institutionalised, they would seem to be well suited as subjects to address Panebianco's challenge to uncover conditions under which such successes may be possible. Our analysis suggests that two factors were particularly important in overcoming these parties' 'charismatic' origins: (1) the timing of the absence of the original leaders and (2) the nature of their replacements.

But since we have suggested the latter two factors were critical for these parties' overcoming *all three* natural pitfalls for right-wing protest parties (origins, message, *and* leadership), it is important that we deal in some detail with the topic of leadership as it relates to institutionalisability of parties. More specifically, it is our purpose in the next chapter to develop a theoretical framework covering the changing leadership needs of parties of entrepreneurial origins as they move through phases of the institutionalisation process. It is our contention that meeting the changing leadership needs is both difficult and critical for survival of the party, and hence why so many fail and so few succeed.[6] Then, in chapter 7, the theory will be applied to the experiences of the Progress parties.

NOTES

1. The founding date for Anders Lange's party was 8 April 1973, and Hagen left the party in July 1974.
2. In contrast, the 1995 split of Kjærsgaard and others from the Danish party – which will be discussed in detail in chapter 8 – was not over organisational strategy so much as over political strategy, that is, whether to seek influence through cooperation with other parties.

3. In the *Handbook for Folketinget 1973* (Folketingets 1973: 357–365) the party's presentation includes positions on not just the three main points, but also such issues as radical constitutional reforms, environmental protection, and social security reforms. The same is true for the party's 1977 programme (see Glistrup 1978).

4. The argument of this paragraph – and many of these words – were first developed by Harmel and Gibson (1995).

5. As noted earlier (see footnote 3), Glistrup had developed more broadly ranging programmes on paper, but the party did not actually run in its early elections on issues other than its three main points of opposition to the status quo. And Glistrup himself, in spite of having been the author of the broader statements, was perceived (and in fact, quoted) as feeling that a general programme was unnecessary.

6. Bolleyer counts thirteen of twenty-five right-wing parties failing to outlive the parties' founder (Bolleyer 2013: 151–152). For examples of parties which did not adequately meet the changing leadership needs and hence did not survive, see Wørlund and Svåsand (2001) and Svåsand and Wørlund (2005) on New Democracy in Sweden and de Lange and Art (2011) on List Pim Fortuyn in the Netherlands.

Chapter 6

Leadership and Institutionalisation of Entrepreneurial Protest Parties

The main underlying assumption of the theoretical framework developed in this chapter[1] is that political parties of entrepreneurial origins develop through three phases on their way from birth to becoming 'parties of relevance' (Sartori 1976). Built upon this assumption, the two main contentions of the framework are: (1) each phase requires somewhat different leadership skills/ orientations and (2) parties will suffer for failing to match leadership abilities to leadership needs at each of the three phases.

We begin with a review of relevant literature on political leadership, which we will then adopt, adapt, and supplement in developing the thesis of different leadership needs at three stages of party development. In chapter 7, we apply the resulting theory to the two Progress parties.

RELEVANT LITERATURE ON LEADERSHIP

The idea that different situations require different leadership skills/orientations is hardly new; in fact, it is a prominent theme within the literature on political leadership.[2] Though the concept of 'changing leadership needs within a given organisation' is not completely absent from this literature (as documented below), the bulk of it refers to different needs across different organisations, or across different levels of the same organisation.

Katz (1973), for instance, develops the thesis that different types and mixes of 'task-oriented' and 'social-emotionally oriented' orientations and behaviour are required for three different levels within a hierarchically structured organisation, with the levels distinguished primarily by the extent to which leaders are given 'freedom' and decision-making latitude (see Table 6.1). Katz asserts, among other things:

At the lower levels in social and political structure (for instance, the precinct captain or ward boss in the political party or the first line supervisor in industry), the area of freedom ... is narrowly circumscribed. ... The skill of the leader lies in assessing what constitutes positive reinforcement for the different members of his group. ... They are not in a position to elaborate or modify system requirements.

At intermediate levels in the organisational structure, the scope for the exertion of influence expands greatly. Task orientation can now go beyond the completion of a given job and can take the form of extending and developing the organisational structure itself ... the special skill of initiative and of innovation ... they have considerable freedom in developing the social-emotional function of adjudication and the engineering of consent. Claims and demands from the subsystems they manage have to be met in some fashion that will ensure the loyalty and effective support of the various groups involved. ... One procedure ... is to develop a two-way orientation in the system, so that he can be representative of those below him and yet accepted by his superiors...

When we reach the top echelons in a social system, the area of freedom for the exercise of influence is greater than at any other level. ... The qualities necessary for leadership at the top levels of complex organisations are heavily conceptual and intellectual ... cognitive skills of a high order. ... The socioemotional pattern at top levels can be one of charisma. (211–215)

Though Katz deals with levels of a single organisation at one point in time, much of his thinking can be applied also to an organisation as it develops over time. Just as the levels can be distinguished on the basis of the unrestrained latitude given to leaders (with the greatest freedom at the top levels), so can the stages of party development (i.e. with much *more* latitude at the party's birth than after the party has become fully institutionalised). In other words, the period of a party's origin would most closely correspond to Katz's upper echelons, and the period after institutionalisation is complete would correspond to his lower levels.

Katz further distinguishes leadership in a 'structured institutional setting' from leadership of a 'relatively unorganised aggregate ... or even a social movement'. While the leader of the already complex organisation is advantaged by greater cohesion, more formal legitimacy, and the presence of sanctions for failing to do his bidding, and has 'better access to mass media, greater resources and staff, and many dependent subgroups', the leaders of loose social movements 'are free to make up their own rules as they go along' and have 'the advantage of the vitality of a new cause, a new formulation of goals'. Katz adds:

Ideology and charisma are more important for the social movement than for the leadership of the ongoing organisation. In the ongoing institution, ideological

Table 6.1   Hierarchical Level and Leadership Patterns

Hierarchical Level in Structured System	*Type of Leadership Process*	*Related Task Orientation*	*Related Socio-emotional Orientation*
Lower levels	administration; use of existing structure	a. technical expertise b. knowledge of rules (non-political)	concern with equity for subordinates
Intermediate levels	extending, supplementing and piecing out of structure	a. insight into organisational problem b. assessment of bargaining possibilities	complex human-relations skill in integrating primary- and secondary-group relations
Top echelon	origination and change of structure; formulation and implementation of new policy	a. system perspective b. originality and creativity	charisma a. symbolic b. authoritarian c. functional

Reproduced from Katz (1973: 212)

leadership can be significant, but it is more a clarification and extension of existing goals than the formulation of new doctrine. (221)

Though parties of external leadership origins do not, by definition, develop from social movements, they do, obviously, begin without an ongoing organisation. Hence, what Katz suggests about the need, early on, for ideology (or at least, 'cause') and charisma, and their declining importance as the organisation matures, has relevance for a theory of changing leadership needs during party development.

Another student of political leadership, Margaret Hermann (1986), argues that 'in striving to co-align and relate to their constituents', political leaders are expected to perform in seven roles: consensus builder, policy advocate, motivator, advertiser, recruiter, listener, and manager; with the major tools for doing so being 'persuasion and bargaining' (borrowed from Neustadt 1960). (She also notes, however, that some of the roles may be delegated by the main leaders to others in the organisation; see Hermann 1986: 183.) In order to fully understand how these roles and tools are used, she argues, one must have a knowledge of a number of features of the context/setting (among other things, of course); including the extent to which decision-making is governed by formalised rules, whether means of resolving internal differences are already in place, the nature of relevant belief systems and norms, and the extent to which the leaders have immediate control over resources.

Immediate control over resources will, for instance, allow leaders to be demanding, prescriptive, and inflexible; whereas the need to win access to resources will require leadership marked by 'consensus seeking, coalition building, compromise, and other conflict resolution techniques' (Hermann 1986: 172).

Though Hermann herself does not deal at length with the notion of the context changing within a given organisation over time, she clearly believes that different types of leadership skills are required in different situations. She notes:

> There is a growing debate over whether the skills learned in one type of political position transfer to another. ... Are the skills needed to run a political campaign the same as the skills needed to govern? Are the skills developed as a revolutionary similar to those needed to form and maintain a government? ... The author has found that the very skills that enabled certain African leaders to be good revolutionaries in the struggle for independence often hindered them in their attempts to govern their new countries. (Hermann 1983: 178)

Furthermore, Hermann argues not only that different situations require different leadership skills, and that not all leaders have all such skills, but also that 'leaders' motives will drive them to seek political leadership positions that provide the opportunity for satisfying their needs', and that

> it is tempting at this point to suggest that political leaders fail or leave office at least partly because their motives are no longer compatible with the leadership position. The leader may have misperceived the opportunity, *the situation may have changed with time*, the needs and interests of those being led may have changed, or the leader's own needs may be different. (176; emphasis added)

Clearly, Hermann's thinking would seem to apply to political parties as they mature from birth (a time of great freedom for leaders to develop programmes and control resources) to institutionalisation (with its routinisation, need for delegating authority, and less direct control over resources). Similarly, it would seem to apply to the success and behaviour of leaders who were drawn to the first situation, but who eventually are faced with the latter one.

Though Katz's and Hermann's works are clearly relevant to the building of a theory of changing leadership needs in developing parties, they are less directly so than two literatures which have focused on changing leadership needs in other contexts: revolutions and social movements. The literature on revolutionary leadership is well summarised by Burns (1978: 202), who notes that 'rare is the revolutionary leader who helps initiate the revolution, lasts through the whole revolutionary cycle of struggle, victory, and consolidation of power, and directs the process of social transformation. ... More often other leaders come to the fore to play their parts during the succeeding stages of the revolutionary cycle'. His point is well illustrated with the case of Martin Luther:

> Luther showed himself to be a master preacher and propagandist. He was not an organiser, a collective leader, a revolutionary strategist. He was more of a prophet than a politician. Master organisers would follow, and then the religious and political armies would march. (205)

In summarising the literature on leadership of social movements, Stein (1971) suggests that the initial leaders of social movements require the skills of preachers, and that the need for organisational skills comes later. With regard to his own framework of three broad phases in the development of political movement, he argues that the first phase of mobilisation and rapid growth in membership requires 'prophets or men of words'; the second phase of consolidation when emphasis is placed on achievements requires 'administrators or agitators'; and the third phase of stabilisation or institutionalisation requires 'statesmen or pragmatic politicians'. The authority of the men of words rests 'either on their recognised superiority as interpreters of the faith or on their qualities as agitators and diffusers of the movement's message or both'; while that of the administrators rests on 'their ability to translate the ideas of the movement into practical forms of action and their capacity for maintaining unity of purpose and coordination, financial support, and enthusiastic devotion and service to the movement'; and that of the statesmen on 'their success in maintaining power or political support for the movement through negotiation, refined strategies and tactics, and pragmatic compromises' (Stein 1971: 15). The emphasis of the first phase is on growth, and once that is achieved the emphasis in the second phase shifts to organisation, and then after the movement has acquired 'a certain stability and legitimacy' the emphasis shifts in the third and final phase to institutionalisation. The latter may, according to Stein, take the form of a political party, though that will not necessarily be the case.

Though there is much that can (and will) be borrowed from Stein's analysis of social movements for our similar analysis of stages in the development of political parties, it must be noted that the differences between the two situations are not insignificant. First and most importantly, a party at its very inception is about the business of electing members into government posts (which is, after all, the defining characteristic of parties), and according to Stein's analysis, social movements will not pursue that goal (if ever) until the third phase of the movement's development. This is particularly important for leadership theory because the party, if and when it is successful in electing members to government, will quite naturally subdivide into 'electoral' and 'governmental' components, each of which may develop and maintain its own leadership. It is possible that the same people will be tapped for leadership of both parts of the party, but this is not necessarily the case; when the two 'fractions' have different leaders, it is obvious that the game of leadership becomes substantially more complex. Even when both units are led by the same person, each of the office holders him/herself has the potential to become an alternative party spokesperson or at least act in an independent fashion; this is particularly true for local office holders. The latter situation, unique to political parties, exaggerates the need for 'controls' that would be necessary in any growing organisation.

A second and related difference between a political party and a social movement is the time frame over which development takes place. Social movements generally develop, quite literally, over generations. One is not necessarily speaking figuratively in saying that one generation of leaders is replaced by 'another *generation* with different ideas'. The timetable for development of a political party is, of course, quite variable, but it is not an exaggeration to say that many parties have developed from their origins to institutionalisation over the span of just four or five elections (roughly fifteen to twenty years). This may serve to complicate the process of keeping the styles of the leaders in sync with the rapidly changing needs of the party. Party founders may be found 'obsolete' long before they consider their generation to be ready for replacement.

And a third important difference between social movements and entrepreneurial parties is that the former tend to have ready-made constituencies, normally identifiable by shared social characteristics (e.g. 'class'), while the latter must build a constituency 'from scratch' on the basis of effective delivery of their message. This means that in the earliest years of development a social movement is concerned with mobilising its existing constituency, while the entrepreneurial party must spend its first years developing an identity that will allow potential supporters to find it. Though both entities are certainly interested from the outset with growth, it is probably fair to say that growth – as a primary focus – must wait until the second stage of party development, while occupying centre stage in the first phase of the movement. For these reasons, it is not possible to simply adopt Stein's analytical framework and apply it directly to political parties.

But with all of these caveats in mind, and though none of the above literature deals directly with party change, it is nevertheless possible to draw heavily from all of it in building a theory of changing leadership needs during several phases of party development. But before doing so, we turn next to discussion of what we have identified as the three most important stages (paralleling those of a social movement to a large degree) in the development of a *party* with external leadership origins.

THREE STAGES OF PARTY DEVELOPMENT

Based on our reading of literatures on leadership (including the items mentioned above) and political party development, it is a mainstay of our framework that the development of the entrepreneurial party, from its inception in the mind of one person to complete institutionalisation, covers various phases. Each phase offers particular opportunities for influencing the political system, and each also requires particular types of leadership skills to deal with its special challenges. The three most important phases in the development of the entrepreneurial party are: first, the period of developing a message and establishing identification; second, the period of organisation and electoral growth; and third, the period of stabilisation when the emphasis is on establishing the party's credibility as well as dependability. From this point on, we will refer to these periods as the identification, organisation, and stabilisation phases of party development.[3] (Though we don't wish to imply that the three dimensions of institutionalisation conform completely to the three phases of the process, we would be remiss not to acknowledge that *routinisation* and *internal value infusion* are included in 'organisation', and *external perceptions* are an important focus of 'stabilisation'.)

Though it is not possible to pinpoint exactly when each phase begins (except, perhaps, the first), a few general guidelines apply. The first period begins, obviously, when the founder of the party declares to at least one other person that he or she is starting a party. Though the first phase continues through the election of the first few representatives of the party in parliament, the second phase begins when the number of parliamentary representatives exceeds a 'handful', and/or when a number of the party's members have been elected to local offices. The second period ends and the third begins when someone, either inside or outside the party, first takes seriously the possibility that the party will/may/could conceivably become a legitimate party for others to cooperate with, whether or not as a coalition partner. Though this treatment has assumed thus far that the three phases are mutually exclusive and follow one another in a particular sequence, it is possible that more than one phase will occur simultaneously. It is our assumption, however, that it is the 'normal' pattern for the phases to follow in sequence, and that simultaneous occurrence significantly complicates the leadership game (as will be illustrated below with the Danish case).

During the identification phase the new party's most important tasks are to develop and communicate its message, whatever that is to be. A new party may attract followers because of its ideas, because of its leader, because it offers the possibility of protest against established parties, or simply because it is new (and perhaps therefore offers greater possibilities for being meaningfully involved); but it can't attract any supporters if they don't know that it exists, and it is not likely to attract many if they don't know what it stands for (or against, as the case may be). Furthermore, the new party is likely to attract attention in proportion to its distinctiveness from other parties, because of its issue positions and/or its organisational style. Attention to the party will then be enhanced to the extent that the leader draws attention to him/herself (whether by charisma or simply 'notoriety') and thereby to the party and its message as well. Though the party's message and style are likely to be altered many times during a long lifetime, it is in the first phase of party development that the party is given its identity and its image, distinguishing it from the other parties in the system. This involves both shaping the party's message, and then delivering it to a substantial number of the public in an effective manner. Though any new entrepreneurial party will hope to draw enough votes in its first election to seat at least its leader in parliament, the greatest emphasis in the first phase (which may in fact be completed prior to the first electoral campaign, though this would not normally be the case) must be upon developing an identification, and with it a loyal cadre of supporters/members for the leader, rather than building electoral machinery (i.e. party organisation) across many constituencies. The party will be heavily dependent upon the drawing power of its leader for any electoral success during this period.

In the first phase of party development, few demands are placed upon the party and few visible actions are taken for it other than by its leader. That situation is likely to change when the party has elected numerous members of parliament and/or local office holders. Office holders, and perhaps especially those at the local levels, may publicly take actions or make statements that are contrary to the wishes of the leader and to the stated positions of the party; this is especially likely in a party that lacks the rules and disciplinary procedures for debate, compromise, and 'internal' resolution of disagreements, that presumably come with routinisation. Hence, during the second phase of party development, emphasis will be placed on establishing the routinised mechanisms of 'control' that were not necessary in the first phase, when only the leader and perhaps a few others represented the party in parliament. Also, demands from below for development of electoral organisation are likely to arise during this second phase, as the taste of electoral success creates an appetite for more. In addition, the presence of many office holders and, presumably, now also a growing number of party members eager to participate, will create demands for delegation of responsibility, that is, for 'meaningful work'. The party that began largely as a one-person operation becomes, in the second phase, a value-infused (or -infusing) organisation with many heads, hands, and voices requiring coordination.

The second phase is also likely to be marked by factionalism that did not exist (or was not so visible) in the first period.[4] As the party grows, resentments may arise between the 'old timers' and the 'new kids on the block'. This is especially likely when newer members/officeholders prefer a 'more pragmatic/normal' approach for growth, at the expense of abandoning some of the party's original message and/or style. Hence, while primary emphasis in the second phase is on the building of a routinised and encompassing organisation, attention to building and maintaining consensus may also be required.

Once a party has gained enough quantitative importance to be recognised by other parties as a potential player in the game of policy-making, it must shift its primary focus away from internal organisation, per se, and towards solidifying a reputation as credible and dependable (or in a word, 'stable'). This will be true irrespective of whether the original impetus is generated by other parties or within the new party itself, and whether other parties' original assessments were favourable or not. (In fact, demands for stabilisation will be greatest in the party whose own members want inclusion in a government, but whose most likely partners have found it unacceptable.) It is during the third phase, then, that the institutionalisation of the party is completed. By this time, the party is likely to have developed sufficient longevity to defy being labelled a 'flash in the pan' and sufficient organisation to be considered 'routinised'; what it lacks is a proven record of ability to contribute to policy-making that will lend stability to its image in the minds of both the electorate and other parties. The bold steps required in the first two phases of party development are now replaced by the need for fine-tuning and implementation of the party's message and procedures, and for achieving a reputation for credibility and reliability among the upper echelons of other parties.

LEADERSHIP NEEDS AND PHASES
OF PARTY DEVELOPMENT

Armed with both the leadership literature summarised above and the description of the three phases of party development just discussed, it is now possible to offer some building material for a theory of changing leadership needs during the development of an entrepreneurial protest party. Table 6.2 summarises the argument, which is based on the idea that each phase has a distinctive primary objective, coupled with a distinctive set of specific tasks, which in turn corresponds to a distinctive set of leadership needs.

Table 6.2 Phases of Party Development

Phase	Primary Objective	Specific Tasks	Leadership Needs
1	Identification	Develop message Communicate message Draw attention to party Adopt (non)organisational style	CREATOR & PREACHER Originality and creativity [Katz; Stein] Communication skills [Burns; Stein] Charisma [Katz] Authoritativeness [Hermann]
2	Organisation	Develop and routinise procedures Delegate and coordinate Develop electoral organisations Build and maintain consensus among competing factions Develop organisational culture	ORGANISER Organisational (and delegational) orientation and skills [Katz] Consensus-building skills [Katz; Hermann] Strategic skills (for growth) [Burns]
3	Stabilisation	Develop reputation for credibility and dependability Fine-tune and implement message and procedures Develop ongoing relations with other parties (perhaps eventually within coalition government)	STABILISER Personal reputation for credibility and dependability Administrative skills (for organisational maintenance and fine-tuning) [Katz] Complex human-relations skills (to lead complex party organisation while dealing with other parties) [Katz; Stein]

During the first phase of party development it is primarily (and in some cases, only) the leader who must shape and effectively communicate the party's message. As the party's founder and, still at this stage, its only visible spokesperson, he or she does so within a context of what Katz might call 'maximum freedom'. The 'originality and creativity' that Katz associates with the top echelon of an established organisation's leadership are needed in the new party as well, for both developing the new party's programme and adopting an organisational approach to see it through the first phase. Needed also are the skills of what Burns labelled (in reference to Luther) the 'master preacher and propagandist' and Stein called (in reference to social movements) a 'diffuser' of the message. But a good message and a good communicator to diffuse it will be for naught if there isn't a 'crowd' to hear it; a leader with charisma, or at least with notoriety, may be able to attract the listeners who will hear the message and associate it not only with the leader, but also with the party. The ideal leader for phase one will combine the qualities of creator, communicator, and charismatic.

But if the leader during the first phase operates within a context of complete freedom, he or she also operates in a vacuum of procedures which would direct others in doing jobs in the fledgling organisation. For this reason, it will help if the leader has an authoritative personality that can be substituted for missing job descriptions and routinised procedures. Hermann (1986) suggests that when the leader has immediate control over resources (which the entrepreneurial party leader certainly does), he/she is allowed to be 'demanding, prescriptive, and inflexible', qualities which may come in handy for the leader of the new and yet unorganised party.

Developing 'the organisation' is the central focus of the second phase of party development, during which the delegation of some of the leader's authority must be instituted as well. In fact, the leader who lacks organisational skills may wish to delegate some of the responsibility for engineering the organisation to someone who is better equipped for that job (à la Hermann 1986: 183). Much more important as a trait of the leader him/herself is an orientation favouring the routinisation of the party's operations. The leader who opposes, as a matter of principle, routinisation at the national level or the development of organisations at the local level – and who shuns value infusion – will be ill-suited for leadership during the second phase.

Other important tasks that develop during the second phase are the development of strategy for further growth (paralleling what Burns says is the revolution's need for strategists once it has moved beyond its first phase), and the building of consensus in what may now be a factionalised organisation. Though the first might be delegated by the leader to someone else, the job of consensus building cannot be easily delegated. Consensus-building skills should be on the resume of the person who plans to lead the party through its second phase of development.

In the third phase, the party must demonstrate to other parties that it would be an acceptable and reliable partner in government (or if that's out of the question, then it must prove that it is at least a 'worthy' opponent). Gone are the days when the party could ask for erratic behaviour to be excused on the grounds of organisational youthfulness. And gone too are the days when the party could benefit from protest against other parties by exaggerating its distinctiveness, if it hopes to be considered 'acceptable' by potential coalition partners. What is needed at the helm during this period is a moderator and stabiliser, someone with good personal credentials for credibility and dependability, and with the skills to diffuse these characteristics throughout the organisation.

Organisation building was the focus of the second phase of development; now what is required in the third phase is maintenance and fine-tuning of what has already been constructed. If phase two was the period of the 'builder', phase three is the period for the 'implementer', requiring what Katz (referring to the lower levels of established organisations) would call 'administrative' skills. The 'grand creator' of the first phase would be likely to find the third phase a poor fit.

Also necessary in the third phase, more so than in the earlier phases, is a leader who can successfully play two games, requiring different roles, simultaneously. As leader of the party, the 'internal' game is played from the top; as negotiator for the party in dealing with others, this 'leader' is just one among equals (at best). What is required is what Katz (referring this time to intermediate levels of established organisations) has succinctly called 'complex human-relations skills'. Not every 'leader' is equipped to play the role of negotiator in a game of peers. The leader of the party in the third phase of its development should be equipped to do both, since neither role can be completely or even substantially delegated to another.

THEORY

Implicit in the idea that the three phases have distinct leadership needs are the related propositions:

1. parties that fail to provide leadership with the requisite skills and orientations at each phase will experience turmoil and eventually collapse; and
2. a party whose leader at one phase lacks the requisite skills and/or orientations for the next phase must either replace or complement that leader with others in order to avoid turmoil and eventual collapse.

The fact that few leaders have all of the skills and orientations required for all three phases, and many lack the skills and orientations for even two of them, means that replacing or complementing leaders is likely to occur in most cases.

When a leader lacks skills which are necessary for a particular phase but which may be delegated, 'complementing' by delegation to sub-leaders may be a suitable alternative to replacing the current leader altogether, but when delegating is not possible, replacement may be the only workable alternative. And because, as Hermann argues, leaders themselves tend to seek out situations where their skills 'fit' and feel awkward when they don't, the change in command may in such cases be voluntary rather than forced. By way of analogy, there is nothing that can more effectively ruin a party (meaning the other kind now) than having a host who clearly is not enjoying herself; the awkwardness that inevitably results can be resolved only by having all of the guests move on to a different setting, or by having the host politely excuse herself and leave. This leads us to the corollary proposition:

3. party leaders who are successful at one phase but who lack the requisite ability and/or desire to continue in the next phase may seek self-fulfilment in other parties whose needs match their particular leadership strengths.

It also follows from the above assumptions and propositions that

4. if more than one phase occurs simultaneously, the tasks of leading and of finding a single leader with all of the requisite skills and orientations (now combining two or more of the sets of needs listed in Table 6.2) become exponentially more complicated.

This could happen, for instance, if a new party elected several representatives in its first election (perhaps due to protest voting against established parties), thereby creating needs for organising and consensus building at a time when the party's own identity must still be established. And at the earliest stage of party development, the founder lacks not only the organisational procedures by which delegation of some of the tasks might otherwise take place, but also the first-hand experience with most followers that will later educate the delegating process (i.e. who can do what, and with what level of confidence?).

In the next chapter, we examine the experiences of the two Progress parties in the light of our framework and these propositions. In spite of their many similarities, including quite similar origins, the parties have followed somewhat different patterns of development, with different 'leadership experiences' and different patterns of institutionalisation as a result. It will be our main contention, however, that both parties provide evidence of the critical role played by the 'right leadership for the right time' in achieving institutionalisation of entrepreneurial parties, including right-wing entrepreneurial protest parties.

NOTES

1. Much of chapters 6 and 7 is taken directly from Harmel and Svåsand (1993).
2. Note that we use the term 'leadership style' as an umbrella to cover both 'skills' and 'orientations'. The term 'skills' is synonymous with 'abilities' and 'orientations' with 'desires'. A person may have the skills (or abilities) to be leader in a particular situation while lacking the orientation (or desire) to do so, and vice versa; in either case, that person would lack the necessary leadership style.
3. In chapter 8 we will suggest that managing political parties in decline (i.e. potentially undergoing 'de-institutionalisation') could require yet another type of leadership skills.
4. During the first phase, those who would disagree strongly with the leader are more likely to leave voluntarily or to be expelled by the leader.

Chapter 7

The Leadership Theory and the Progress Parties

In this chapter, we apply the leadership-and-institutionalisation theory developed in chapter 6 to the two Progress parties, both of which clearly began as entrepreneurial protest parties. Though the Danish party was actually founded before the Norwegian party and to some extent served as its model, we begin these case analyses with the Norwegian party because it lends itself to a somewhat more straightforward application of the framework outlined above.

THE NORWEGIAN PROGRESS PARTY

Phase One: Identification

In 1973, when sixty-nine-year-old Anders Lange founded his 'Anders Lange's Party for a Strong Reduction in Taxes, Rates, and Public Intervention', he did not have a resume full of political experience and governmental office-holding, though this dog kennel owner had used the pages of his dog owners' newsletter to present his political arguments,[1] and he had been a long-time member of the Conservative Party (Høyre). He also had his short list of issue positions that clearly set him apart from the existing parties (including the Conservatives), and his orientation towards 'normal party organisation' that would only enhance the distinctiveness of his new party. What he lacked in skills of polished speaking, he seemingly made up for with a knack for doing things that were designed to bring attention to himself. And whatever he may have lacked in ability to formulate a grand ideology, he made up for with the ability to articulate (albeit and importantly in 'everyday' language) a few arguments on points that reached a significant number of Norwegians 'where they were at' in the early 1970s.

The platform that Lange developed for his party for its first election campaign in 1973 consisted of a single sheet of paper listing on one side the ten things that the party was 'tired of' and on the other side the ten things that it was 'for'. Perhaps better than a multi-paged manifesto could have done, Lange's list used a minimum of words to strike home with a large number of 'average Norwegian tax-payers', his target audience. His one sheet challenged not only 'taxes', but also some fundamental aspects of the welfare state (which, he could argue effectively, was not being done by any other party).[2]

The transcript of Lange's address to the founding meeting in the Oslo theatre clearly shows that he was not a 'polished' speaker. The talk was a lengthy, rambling oration that included anecdotes ranging from the price of coffee in the Storting cafeteria to many of his personal experiences. But the talk was high on entertainment value, the personal stories were ones the audience could relate to and were usually tied to a point that Lange was making, and the important issues – taxes being too high, excessive foreign aid, misuse of social security funds, meddling of the government in use of alcohol and tobacco – were all covered by the talk's end. No one could have left the theatre unconvinced of Lange's intention to be different from 'the political boys of this country' (one derogatory reference among many to the 'established politicians') and to lead a party very different from the rest.

And whatever the message consisted of, Lange was quite willing to make a spectacle of himself in order to assure that it would get a substantial hearing. Wearing a toy sword and drinking egg liqueur during a nationally televised debate, as Lange did in 1973, is hardly destined – or intended – to go unnoticed.[3]

Not only would the message and the medium be unique, but the organisation would be as well. Lange clearly was oriented against complex party organisation. Feeling that organisation always meant an unresponsive 'top', Lange instead preferred the 'spontaneous action' that was possible only in a loose movement. He punctuated this philosophical opposition to normal party organisation by associating it, sarcastically, with the '*gammelpartiene*' ('old-time parties') of the establishment from which he sought to distance himself. Thus, by choosing an organisational approach that was unique among Norwegian parties, Lange willingly exaggerated the distinctiveness the party already enjoyed for its issue positions.

Though Lange had and exercised the freedom to choose the original (anti-) organisational approach himself, the dispute that was soon to arise with Carl I. Hagen over that choice would give Lange the opportunity to show that he had and would use considerable authority as well. Within two years of the party's founding, Hagen's pro-organisation faction left the party specifically because of Lange's refusal to compromise on that point.

If Lange had the skills, or at least the 'instincts' and orientations, to be a successful party *creator and preacher*, it is also clear that he lacked the

Figure 7.1 Anders Lange smokes a pipe and drinks egg liqueur during a televised debate on 7 September 1973 at the Norwegian Public Broadcasting Corporation prior to the elections. According to the newspaper *Stavanger Aftenblad*, '[Lange] brought a toy sword to demonstrate that now "taxes, fees and public interventions" would be cut'. (http://www.aftenbladet.no/meninger/kommentar/Anders-Lange_-en-glemt-naturverner-532052b.html) *Credit:* NTB Scanpix.

necessary skills and orientations to be a successful *organiser* in the second phase of the party's development. His strongly felt orientation against complex organisation speaks for itself; the very visible split from the party suggests a possible weakness in the consensus-building area as well. Whether serious difficulties and eventual leadership replacement would have resulted during the second phase is impossible to determine, since Lange died on 18 October 1974, less than two years after the party's birth.

For the next three years, the party selected leaders who were among Lange's original supporters, but who were neither preachers nor organisers, and the party fell into electoral decline – losing all seats in parliament in the 1977 election (down from the four seats in the debut 1973 election). But Hagen – a young man with personal charisma and with pro-organisational orientation and skills – had been waiting in the wings since his return to the party in 1975, and in 1978 he was selected as the party's leader. Hagen's ascent marked the beginning of the second phase of the Norwegian Progress Party's development.

Phase Two: Organisation

When Carl I. Hagen was enlisted into Lange's 'movement' at its first meeting in the Oslo theatre in 1973, little could he have surmised that only weeks later he would find himself in the informal position of party secretary, or that in 1974 he would be leading a highly visible split from Lange that would result in yet another new party. And when he led his troops out, he could not have envisioned that a few months later Lange would be dead, and that in 1978 he himself would be selected to lead the remnants of Lange's little movement.

Though Hagen has often been called the most charismatic figure in Norwegian politics, both the style and the instincts that he brought to the top position in Progress (as the party had been renamed in 1977) were clearly more 'normal' than Lange's had been. Hagen was a man of well-tailored suits, not swords. And his organisational orientation, shaped as a student of marketing in London and as a keen observer of politics in Norway's established and 'successful' parties, was to stress the distinctiveness of his party's *product*, rather than the unique ways in which it was packaged and sold. The programme, the means of communicating it, and the party's organisation all became foci for Hagen's penchant for normalcy.

The positions of the party on its 'main points' ('strong reduction in taxes, rates, and public intervention') would not be altered, but its programme would be expanded to cover virtually all major political issues, resulting by 1989 in a ninety-page, slickly printed and bound document. Though the inspiration for the expanded programme came from Hagen himself, its contents were now developed and adopted at a party convention, not exclusively in the mind of the leader as had been the case under Lange. The latter difference did not occur by accident, but was instead by Hagen's design. For Hagen, the desire to build a normal, member-based organisation meant that members would need to be included in the party's decision-making processes, including those related to the manifesto.

> If you want to have a lot of people working together to achieve a victory or seats in Parliament or local city councils, in our day and age it's impossible to get people involved with fighting this battle unless they also have some say. ... they have to be part of the decision making. In other words, you have to have a system whereby you make a manifesto ... and you can only do that through an organisation that is built like an ordinary, traditional party organisation. (From Hagen interview with Harmel, 1988)

By the early 1980s, the party had developed extra-parliamentary organisation at the national level that was similar to its more established counterparts, was actively encouraging the development of organisation at the local levels, and had in general 'routinised' many of the procedures that Lange would clearly have preferred to leave 'loose' (see Harmel and Svåsand 1989).

The changes did not come without cost to party unity. One faction, with many of Hagen's own recruits at its core, supported the march towards normalcy, but many of the 'old-timers' who had been enlisted into Lange's original movement resisted the changes. Hagen, recognising that he needed both the old and the new supporters in order to win elections and in order to avoid visible wrangling and departures that would hurt the party's image, encouraged the forces of change behind the scenes while developing an image of even-handedness on the main stage.

> I rather have the two extremes both unhappy, but satisfied, rather than let one extreme win. That is my form of ... leadership. When you lead a big movement you can't let the [one] extreme win, because then the other extreme is going to leave you and make a lot of noise. Arguing gradually and having debates [is my preference]. (From Hagen interview with Harmel, 1988)

As the party grew during the second phase, Hagen himself seemingly recognised the needs and opportunities to adapt his leadership style:

> It's a different form of leadership running a shop with 7 employees or 100 employees than running a company with 2,000 employees; that's the same in the political process. Now I can give guidelines in general terms; I can give advice; I can try to be a good example, try to be inspired. But it's indirect leadership more through signals rather than telling individual people what to do and what not to do. ... That's one thing which is important.

> [On the other hand,] 'controlling' is important to stop people or representatives from really going against our political platform; it's very important as an organisation ... [that now has] 800 members of local city councils and county councils ... [and] another 1,500 filling places on boards and committees, and so on. ... Now, our competitors are very quick to pick up on one of these if they do exactly opposite of what is stated in our party political platform. ... So, we have a controlling role centrally in overseeing or overviewing that. And if we get examples [of that we should] take action [on] and 'take action' is to talk to that local party, trying to understand that this was not the right thing to do. So it's the leadership of preservation and talking and arguing rather than telling, because telling people tends to get them in a defensive position, and they will fight rather than try to get an agreement. (From Hagen interview with Harmel, 1988)

During the second phase, Hagen had pursued the strategy of developing normal party organisation, platform, and behaviour; while continuing to stress the differences from all other parties on a few important issues, and the strategy seemingly paid off at the ballot box, with a jump from 3.7 per cent of the votes (two seats) in 1985 to 12.8 per cent (twenty-two seats) in 1989. That number of seats, plus the fact that the party had now lasted for sixteen years and through five national elections, meant that the other bourgeois parties might no longer be able to simply 'ignore them and maybe they'll go away'.

Phase Three: Stabilisation

Perhaps the biggest question facing the Progress Party as it marked the end of its second decade was whether Carl I. Hagen was still 'the man for the job'. Though Hagen had for some time been routinising procedures and delegating responsibilities to hand-picked deputy leaders, who presumably were being groomed as possible successors, the facts remained that Hagen continued to be the most visible spokesperson for the party, by far, and that many of the party's voters and members as well as politicos outside Progress continued to wonder whether 'Hagen's party' could survive without him. It was within that context that the third phase arrived.

Of primary concern to a party entering the final phase of institutionalisation is the need to establish the party's stability, not only in terms of credibility but also its reliability, in the eyes of other relevant parties. For a party to succeed at the third stage of institutionalisation, it is critical that it be viewed as a party that is capable of following through on its promises and/or threats. In other words, it must be politically predictable and at least to that extent 'normal'. For the party with ambitions to govern, ultimate success on this dimension might take the form of becoming a viable coalition partner. But for the party which is satisfied with impacting policy while remaining outside of government, it would seem sufficient that other parties feel it necessary to negotiate with the party over critical matters, or at the very least to take its blackmail threats seriously.

As of 1985, when Hagen tipped his hand as the non-socialist government was being formed and declared that his party's two votes could be counted upon, the leaders of the other parties might have taken him at his word but still took a public posture of 'ignoring' Progress. With the party's two votes required in order to keep the new government in power, it might certainly have seemed to some that the other parties' (and especially the centre parties') leaders were ignoring Progress partly over personality differences with Hagen. After all, Hagen's relationship with the leaders of the other parties had so far been one of mutual disdain. Whether a man who had, for more than a decade, attacked his counterparts with a mixture of accusation and ridicule was now well suited for negotiating with them was doubtful at best. Could it be that for the party to fully accomplish its desired negotiating status, it would be necessary for a fresh face to move to the helm? Certainly, that would seem to have been the case unless Hagen was the truly rare individual who could span the leadership needs of all three phases of party development.

It would seem that Hagen was indeed exceptional in this regard. By the 1989 campaign, in spite of Progress's voting with the socialists in bringing down the government, some within the Conservative Party were talking as if it might *sometime* be possible for Progress to be formally involved in a non-socialist coalition. Though that would have to wait for some future government, the 1989 election nonetheless resulted in a minority non-socialist government which did negotiate with Progress – which now held twenty-two seats. The relationship between the new government and the Progress Party was different this time, compared with 1985. The incoming prime minister from the Conservative Party, Jan P. Syse, offered to keep Hagen continuously informed on the government negotiations between the Conservatives, the Christian People's Party, and the Centre Party. Hagen, though, was so displeased over Progress not being invited into the government outright that he turned down that offer.[4] Nevertheless, he still cooperated with the new government on an issue-by-issue basis, and later in the fall he and the Progress Party participated in regular budget negotiations with the government, for the first time ever. Unlike in 1985 – when the parties' agreement was jotted down on a cocktail napkin – this time the budget negotiations involved greater formality, with minutes taken to record the details. In late December, the Progress Party and the government finalised the budget agreement (Hagen 2007: 168–170). Clearly, the leaders of the other parties, in spite of what might have been their personal feelings towards Hagen, recognised that the routinisation of power in the hands of the Progress Party's leader – whether Hagen or some successor – meant that he or she could make promises for the party, and keep them. Thus, by the end of the 1980s the Norwegian Progress Party had achieved the negotiating status – and the stabilisation – that it had desired and that the other parties had for so long withheld. In a very real sense, Hagen had led his party out of political isolation and into their political promised land.[5]

THE DANISH CASE

Phase One: Identification

Lange's job of creating an identity for his brand-new party in Norway may have been eased somewhat by the fact that it was common knowledge that in Denmark, Mogens Glistrup's one-man battle against taxes had already been turned into a new anti-establishment party that was having a remarkable showing in public opinion polls. Glistrup, a lawyer and teacher of tax law, had converted his own lack of political experience and of connections with 'the politicians' into assets, beginning with his first television appearance early in 1971. With his two-minute message equating tax evaders to resistance fighters, Glistrup presented his desired 'hard-boiled egg' (Glistrup 1978). Coming as it did on the weekend when most Danes were completing their own tax returns, his anti-tax message and the way it was presented were bound to become the talk of Copenhagen, if not the entire country.

But to keep his ideas in the public mind beyond the initial splash, Glistrup gave interviews to popular newspapers and magazines and wrote 'letters to the editors' of papers that refused his offer to serve as a political columnist (Glistrup 1978: 3–4). And when he did these things, Glistrup consciously shaped the message to conform to the audience:

> The main purpose of course was to preach a new political message. But when appearing on the public media I had to express myself in simple phrases – contrary to those used by schooled politicians – and even mix the message with characteristics of 'general human interest' like eating marzipan, having a big private swimming pool, day start at 4 a.m., etc. ... The result was that I became publicly well-known and that my most important viewpoints were disseminated at the same time. (Glistrup 1978: 3)

If the main purpose was to preach the message, then a close second was to scare the non-socialist parties into offering him a place on one of their parliamentary slates. When it became clear that would not happen, Glistrup founded his own party instead.

And hence the meeting in Tivoli Gardens in August 1972, when Glistrup told his friends of his plans! His time and attention would now turn to campaigning, since the initial platform had already been written and adopted, by Glistrup himself of course. During the years from 1970 through 1972, Glistrup had single-handedly developed the programme:

> I tried to figure out all political aspects and to build up a platform without any self-contradiction whatsoever. ... it was wonderful to do so on my own without restraint from boards, pressure groups or need for yielding to prejudice within the electorate. (1978: 5)

With a firm grasp of the platform, Glistrup not only continued the interviews and the letter-writing but also now travelled the country giving speeches on behalf of his new party.

The outcome of election day, 4 December 1973, would not only send tremors through Denmark's political landscape, but also would significantly alter the nature of the Progress Party itself. Five new parties together won approximately one-third of the votes; Progress was the biggest of these. In fact, with its 15.9 per cent of the total vote, Progress won 28 seats (of 179 in the Folketing), making it the second-largest party in parliament (Glistrup 1978). Touted as a 'political miracle' by some and labelled a 'fluke' by others, this tremendous victory bore the seeds of what would soon become the beginning of a nightmare for its founder.

Phase Two: Organisation

Glistrup's little party was suddenly quite large, and with its added size (particularly at the level of office holders) came the need for organisation. The party was not yet fully finished with the 'identification' phase, with many of its votes of the 'protest' variety and its overall message not yet clear in the minds of many Danes. Nonetheless, it was suddenly thrust into the 'organisation' phase as well. And this for a party whose leader was already on record (at the first organisational meeting; see Larsen 1978) as strongly opposing organisation at both the national and local levels! As if that were not enough, it would soon become obvious that the parliamentary group contained within it two factions: one supporting Glistrup's 'fundamentalism' the other sponsoring a more 'practical' approach to politics (especially with regard to cooperation with other parties).

The organisational problems were partially solved by delegation. Glistrup, after all, had not (as Lange had) opposed organisation at the local levels so much on principle as on practical grounds; he primarily didn't want to be bothered with it. So those who wanted it badly enough could do it, as far as Glistrup was concerned. As for the national level, organisation would be developed, but it would differ from the other parties by including for its founder a position of leadership for life.

Bigger problems were to be found in the parliamentary group, which was immediately too large for one person to completely dominate, especially since it was also quite diverse. It was possible, after all, for people with many different political orientations to share the three main points of Glistrup's programme. From the outside, Progress was still very much 'Glistrup's party', as he wanted it to be, but inside it was something quite different. Glistrup, who so closely identified with the fundamentalist approach and lacked a personality that would favour the settling of disputes through negotiation, was hardly equipped to build a consensus.[6]

While all of this was going on, Glistrup was having to deal with his own tax problems in the courts. Having declared publicly in 1971 that, in spite of being a millionaire, he paid no taxes; Glistrup was later charged with several tax law violations. In 1978 he was tried and convicted. On 23 February 1981, an intermediate court – after hearing an appeal of the decision – finally sentenced Glistrup to four and a half years in prison (though that term would be cut in half if he also paid a stiff fine). Glistrup appealed again to the High Court, where on 22 June 1983, his sentence was reduced to three and a half years. As is customary in Denmark, he did not actually serve the entire prison sentence, but was jailed from 31 August 1983 through 11 March 1985 (Nielsen 2000: 15, 174).

During Glistrup's absence, leadership would be shared by the parliamentary group chair, Helge Dohrmann, and Glistrup's successor as parliamentary

Figure 7.2 The Danish theatre group Solvognen at a Progress Party rally in 1974. Mogens Glistrup is seated at the table, left of 'Z' poster. *Credit:* Scanpix Denmark; *Photographer:* Gregers Nielsen.

spokesperson, Pia Kjærsgaard. Both Dohrmann (forty-four years old and with background as a construction contractor) and Kjærsgaard (a thirty-six-year-old housewife, home helper,[7] and new member of parliament – actually Glistrup's suppliant, who took his seat upon the imprisonment) were much more organisationally oriented than Glistrup. With Glistrup away, Dohrmann ran the party on a day-to-day basis as Kjærsgaard developed into the party's most popular public face (apart from Glistrup, of course). Together, they attempted to move the party towards greater organisational normalcy than Glistrup had accomplished or favoured. And under their leadership, the party for the first time demonstrated an interest in cooperating with the other non-socialist parties.

However, although Glistrup was out of sight during his prison term, he was never really out of mind. His 'founder's imprint' continued to be felt much more prominently than the absent Lange's in Norway. The situations were different in three important respects: (1) Glistrup was away, but not dead, and so he could still communicate with his followers, (2) Lange had led his party for only one year prior to his death, while Glistrup had been at the helm for more than ten years, and (3) Glistrup was certain to return to a position of leadership in the party, since that was all but guaranteed by its constitution's 'Glistrup clause'.

The years 1987–88 would prove to be very important for the party and for its leadership. On the one hand, Kjærsgaard's shared leadership arrangement with Dohrmann shifted more in her favour after a tremendous electoral performance for which she was given much of the credit. During the campaigns of September 1987 and April 1988, Kjærsgaard was the party's most prominent public face, and when the elections increased the party's number of seats from six to nine and then again to sixteen seats, she would increasingly be seen as its 'saviour'. But on the other hand, Glistrup himself regained a position in the parliament as a result of the 1987 election, and his return to the parliamentary group was certain to fuel tensions between his supporters and Kjærsgaard's. Her attempts to more fully routinise the party so as to alter the party's image, already made difficult by the Glistrup provision and the requirement of an extraordinary majority (2/3) to change any of the rules, would now be all the more difficult with Glistrup's continual presence both in the parliamentary group and the party headquarters. (see also Bille 1987: 17). And while Kjærsgaard and Dohrmann had at least partially succeeded in developing a 'party culture', the continued presence of Glistrup and his followers – who never fully committed to the de-personalisation project – meant potential would remain for de-infusion. (More on that in chapter 8!)

Phase Three: Stabilisation

By the time of Glistrup's return to parliament, the party had clearly moved into its third phase under Dohrmann's and Kjærsgaard's management, but it was still facing unresolved business from the first and second phases that complicated their jobs and threatened to keep the party from becoming fully institutionalised. During the pre-prison era, the party had certainly established identity, and yet the identity 'problem' was not completely settled.

On the one hand, the party did develop a broader programme (largely in spite of Glistrup) and became identified with that programme, but on the other hand the party also continued to be strongly identified with Glistrup, who sometimes expressed quite different views. For instance on defence, Glistrup felt and stated publicly that the defence budget should be greatly reduced and the country should leave NATO, neither of which was a position of the party. In addition, the party was kept from fully routinising by Glistrup's insistence on maintaining the 'Glistrup clause', even throughout his prison term.

While Glistrup had been away, and Dohrmann and Kjærsgaard had been more clearly in charge of the party's day-to-day affairs, the other parties had effectively granted Progress 'coalition potential' status. Beginning in 1981, non-socialist minority governments had seen fit to publicly negotiate with Progress for its support. However, with Glistrup back in parliament, this became even more complicated. Glistrup, with his well-known dislike, resentment, and distrust of 'establishment politicians', lacked both the desire and the ability to perform effectively as a negotiator in dealing with other parties' leaders.

As long as Glistrup remained, the party was in a sort of 'limbo', with uncertain identity (phase 1), organisational approach (phase 2), and place in the system (phase 3). The electorate and the other parties were ready to treat Progress as an institution of Danish politics; the biggest obstacle was the continued presence of the original leadership, well-equipped for founding a party but ill-equipped to lead it through the rest of its development. And, ironically but predictably, the seeds of these problems had been sown in the party's brilliant, debut electoral performance.

In 1989, though, the party – for the first time – entered into an agreement with the governing parties that called for casting all of Progress's votes for the budget bill. Despite the agreement, Glistrup later (in March 1990) cast his vote against a bill that was part of the budget agreement (see Bille 1998: 76), seriously threatening whatever confidence the other parties may have developed in Progress as a partner.

As a direct reaction to Glistrup's vote, in the spring of 1990 the main board – with Kjærsgaard and her supporters now in the majority – adopted a policy that the board would not allow renomination of any member of parliament who had voted against the party line. The journey leading to Glistrup's eventual ousting had begun. In November 1990 the parliamentary group presented Glistrup with an ultimatum: sign a piece of paper saying that he would not break party discipline and would not start another party (as he had threatened on numerous occasions), or suffer expulsion from the

Figure 7.3 Pia Kjærsgaard waving the Danish flag after Denmark voted 'No' to the Maastricht Treaty on 2 June 1992. (Translation of this caption: https://www.b.dk/politiko/perspektiv/nej-sigerne-er-umodne-og-ja-sigerne-arrogante.) Progress Party poster in the background. *Credit:* Scanpix Denmark; *Photographer:* Palle Hedeman.

group. Glistrup refused to sign, and the group expelled him – by an eight to seven vote, with one abstention – and three others who had sided with Glistrup. While not formally resigning from the party and its main board, Glistrup founded a new party called the Well-being Party in time for the December 1990 election. In 1991 the Progress Party's national meeting did something that would have been unthinkable a decade earlier, expelling Glistrup from the party he had founded and then removing the 'Glistrup clause' from the rules with the requisite two-thirds majority. With the departure of Glistrup and Glistrup-related trappings, and with no apparent ramifications for internal stability, the Danish party provided strong evidence of both routinisation and internal value infusion. The party clearly had entered institutionhood.

CONCLUSION

All of the propositions discussed earlier in chapter 6 have gained support from this analysis of the two Progress parties. First (with regard to our 'assumption'), different leadership orientations and skills were found to be associated with each of the three phases of party development. Second (on proposition 1), problems did develop within the Danish party when the skills of the original leader no longer meshed with the needs of a more 'advanced' (i.e. larger) party. Third (on proposition 2), both parties did experience changes of leadership that coincided (somewhat) with the changing leadership needs, sometimes due to 'unrelated' causes and one time due to dismissal. Fourth (on proposition 3), the Danish party provided an example of an individual 'circulating' among parties to fulfil his leadership ambitions (Glistrup to his new Well-being Party when Progress rejected him).[8] And finally (on proposition 4), the Danish party clearly illustrates the complications that arise for leadership and for the party generally when more than one phase occur simultaneously, in this case due to the party becoming 'so big' so soon after being founded.

In more general terms, both cases clearly demonstrate the importance of having 'the right leader for the time'. It is impossible, of course, to know for certain whether Kjærsgaard, or even Hagen, could have done as well as their more flamboyant predecessors during the earliest days and months of party-founding. The fact is, though, that none of the other new parties of the early 1970s in either country (and there were numerous such parties in both countries), all of which had more 'normal' leaders, would do nearly as well in elections. Complicating our ability to assign causality, however, is the fact that none of those other parties had issue profiles anywhere close to those of the two anti-tax parties.

NOTES

1. In the 1930s Lange had been secretary of the right-wing Patriotic League (Fedrelandslaget).

2. As noted in chapter 5, though, neither Progress party ever opposed the welfare state concept in general.

3. Not only did Lange attract attention to himself by doing so; it was also reported that sales of egg liqueur rose dramatically.

4. Hagen would later indicate regret over that decision.

5. Whether it could remain there was still somewhat of an open question. Indeed, challenges to Hagen's own control of the party would come to a head in 1994, raising the possibility of de-institutionalisation of what was by then an institutionalised party. That story awaits in chapter 8.

6. Glistrup himself acknowledged 'always back[ing] out from intrigues' rather than becoming actively involved in the shaping of a compromise (1978: 5), with the consequence that those who disagreed strongly might well be inclined to – and allowed to – leave. Some would dispute this claim of Glistrup's, however. For instance, see Thorndahl 1984.

7. In Denmark, a *hjemehjaelp* is someone who helps the elderly in their homes.

8. As will be noted in chapter 8, Kjærsgaard would also leave the Danish Progress Party in 1995, and immediately start the alternative Danish People's Party.

Part III

DE-INSTITUTIONALISATION

Chapter 8

After Institutionhood

Concept, Theory, and Application of 'De-Institutionalisation'

In earlier chapters, we established that by the early 1990s both Progress parties had reached the status of institutions. Both had demonstrated *objective durability* not only by persisting for more than two decades, but also by surviving several types of shocks, including a name change (the Norwegian party in 1977); splits and other well-publicised resignations (both parties); leadership departures (Lange's death in 1974; Glistrup's trip to prison in 1983–85 for tax evasion); issue encroachment by other parties (both); and electoral disasters (the Danish party dropping to 3.6 per cent of the vote and six seats after a 1973 debut with 15.9 per cent and twenty-eight seats; the Norwegian party winning four seats in its debut but losing all representation at the next election). Both had substantially *de-personalised* and *routinised* their organisations' behaviour, most dramatically after pro-organisation Carl I. Hagen's assumption of the Norwegian party's leadership in 1978 and with the Danish party's dramatic moves to deflate its founder's role in 1991 (including removal of the famous 'Glistrup clause'). As evidence of *external institutionalisation*, both parties had established attached (or 'core') electorates, especially compared to other parties in their own systems. And that they had acquired a measure of respectability in the eyes of other parties was shown as early as 1981 in Denmark when a non-socialist minority government negotiated for Progress's parliamentary support; and began in Norway in 1985 when the non-socialist government formally negotiated for Progress's support for the budget bill.[1]

But that these parties were fully institutionalised by the early 1990s would hardly assure that both would 'live happily ever after'. In a now classic piece on the relationship of political development and modernisation, Huntington (1965: 393) reminded us that institutions 'decay and dissolve as well as grow and mature'. As applied to our subject of entrepreneurial issue parties: a party which routinises behaviour may still choose to abandon the strictures of normal organisational behaviour; a party which de-personalises may come to re-personalise; one which gains respectability with other parties may lose it. It is our contention for the remainder of this chapter that as the Progress parties left their youth behind and entered the next stage of their organisational lives as 'institutions', one was better equipped than the other to handle the occasional setbacks which may, in fact, be quite commonplace among institutionalised parties. The one, equipped with skillful leadership and an organisational milieu within which that leader still enjoyed great flexibility, proved capable of surviving and reversing its isolated instances of decay. The other, laden with both organisational and leadership issues, fell victim to a multifaceted process of institutional decay.

We begin with discussion of the concept 'de-institutionalisation'. Next we detail the experiences of the two Progress parties in their early years of institutionhood, with special reference to their different experiences of institutional decay, and finally develop theory – highlighting but not limited to the role of changing leadership needs – to help explain those experiences.

THE CONCEPT OF *DE-INSTITUTIONALISATION*

Though Huntington (1965) was not explicit in defining 'decay', it can be inferred from his use of the term that it included, as at least one aspect, the breakdown of organisations that were already institutionalising, if not fully institutionalised.

In more general usage, the term 'decay' is taken as synonymous with deterioration, decomposition, or disintegration. As applied to a living organism, decay implies that some wound has not been effectively treated, such that decomposition has begun. Even after decay has set in, however, it is often possible to remove and/or arrest the deterioration. To do so most often requires first the removal of the affected tissue, followed by vigorous treatment with medication. But if the original onset of decay is left untreated or treated ineffectively, the likely result is a spreading of the decay to include other limbs or organs, and eventually general decomposition of the body.

For our purposes, which involve applying the concept to the deterioration of party organisations, 'decay' will be equated explicitly with 'de-institutionalisation'. As such, de-institutionalisation may occur as discrete setbacks during the process of institutionalisation, or as isolated instances of reversal when the organisation is fully institutionalised. Beyond that, it may also occur as a set of related setbacks or reversals, that is, as a 'process' of de-institutionalisation. Just as isolated instances of setback or reversal may themselves be arrested or reversed by skilful organisational leaders, ineffectively or untreated instances may develop into a full-blown process of de-institutionalisation.

With de-institutionalisation defined as the deterioration of institutionalisation, we take as evidence any clear signs of reversal from our indicators for institutionalisation, on any or all of the separate dimensions.

Internal De-institutionalisation

Ignoring established patterns of behaviour – and replacing the established patterns with ad hoc decision-making – is evidence of de-routinisation. While reverting from behaviour based in established rules/norms to decision-making by a single leader of the moment would be an example, re-personalising the party's organisation is only one of the forms this de-routinisation might take. Replacing accepted routines by ad hoc practices is the key; 'changing' existing patterns to new, regularised patterns – if done according to written rules or unwritten party norms – would not be evidence of de-institutionalisation.[2] In fact, changes from old routines to new ones could be taken as further evidence of *institutionalised* organisation, where regularised application of rules and norms continues to be valued.

Evidence of de-routinisation could obviously come in many forms. Just a couple of examples would include the holding (or not holding) of party meetings or the expulsion of members without following accepted procedures.

Decline in internal value infusion would also indicate internal de-institutionalisation. Indirect indicators of potential trouble in this area would include marked declines in party membership or marked increases in defections of party representatives. Whereas such events occurring after departure of the founding leader may be taken as evidence that internal value infusion has not yet occurred, the same events occurring after departure of some later party leader could signal de-infusion of value associated with 'the party in its own right'.[3]

External De-institutionalisation

Just as external institutionalisation takes the form of perceptions by external observers – including in particular voters and other parties – that the party is not just a 'flash in the pan' and has relevance for future planning, de-institutionalisation involves loss of such perceptions. Behavioural evidence of de-institutionalisation from the perspective of the electorate would come in the form of loss – and absence of replacement in the relatively short term – of a stable core electorate. From the perspective of other parties of relevance, de-institutionalisation would be evidenced in their growing disregard for the party, for example, no longer granting the party either coalition or blackmail potential. While the denigration may well be due to altered perceptions of the likelihood the party will continue to exist for the foreseeable future, the reason for the changed perceptions of relevance is less important than the perceptual – and consequent behavioural – changes themselves.

Loss of Objective Durability

As one indicator of the durability dimension of *institutionalisation*, growing 'persistence' is operationalised as gradual increases in age. But when it comes to *de-institutionalisation*, decline in persistence is an abrupt event, ultimately marked at the instant when the party ceases to exist. While going beyond simple electoral failure, party death may still take different forms in different contexts, including de-registration, declaration of cessation by party leadership and/or party conference, or being subsumed into a merger where the former party effectively loses both form and identity.

For the other aspect of durability, survivability, decline is less categorical. For this aspect, de-institutionalisation is evidenced in the inability of the party to cope with either an internal or external shock. Though clearly indicating a weakening or 'decline' of the party as institution, failure to cope with a single shock will not necessarily result in its demise.

In sum, then, evidence of de-institutionalisation would include

1. important decisions being made by behaviour which defies routinised rules, and yet that are allowed to stand;
2. indications of re-personalisation of the party;
3. instability or decline in the party's *core* electorate;
4. evidence of decline in the party's blackmail/coalition potential (as seen through statements or behaviour of other parties) due to other than simply decline in votes and/or seats;
5. evidence of decline in the party's ability to cope with internal or external 'shocks'.

It should be noted that while we have included in our indicators several measures involving 'decline' – that is, in the core electorate, the blackmail/coalition potential, and ability to survive shocks – we have been careful not to directly equate decay with 'electoral decline'. The latter term is reserved for negative trends regarding the party's achievement of electoral goals. Most often, a party is said to be in 'decline' when it is experiencing – over a series of elections – diminishing shares of votes and/or seats. Such a decline may indeed serve as a 'challenge' to the party and its leaders, causing them to rethink aspects of the party's organisation or public profile. The same may be true for discrete disturbances to the party's system, such as death of a popular leader or the birth of a rival party. But the fact that a party is challenged does not mean that it will necessarily fall into decay. In fact, there are many examples in party history of parties facing challenges and remaining relatively healthy, if not even stronger than before.[4] Indeed, we have gone so far as to treat such experiences as indicators of survivability, one aspect of institutionalisation itself. It is not the *challenge* which serves as evidence of institutionalisation or de-institutionalisation, but rather the character of the response from leaders or relevant others within or outside the party.

THEORETICAL IMPLICATIONS: FACTORS IN DE-INSTITUTIONALISATION

As noted above, the three separable dimensions or 'types' of *institutionalisation* can be theoretically linked in various ways. Separate aspects of *de-institutionalisation* may also be theoretically related to one another, sometimes simply as reversals of the hypothesised links between dimensions of institutionalisation. Whereas routinisation can contribute to both external institutionalisation and objective durability, for instance; de-routinisation – for example, when involved with re-personalisation – may well contribute to a reduction in outsiders' perceptions that the party is still trustworthy, and could ultimately threaten its continued durability.

But again, as with institutionalisation, a complete understanding of de-institutionalisation must certainly take other factors into account as well, though those 'other factors' may not impact all of the three dimensions. De-routinisation is likely to be driven by internal factors having little to do with the other components of de-institutionalisation; leadership replacement is one prominent suspect. Electoral decline and critical policy shifts are two likely factors in external de-institutionalisation. We have indicated that persisting through 'shocks' is an indicator of survivability and thus objective durability; however, following the same reasoning, multiple shocks in close proximity could challenge a party beyond its ability to cope, and thus be a factor in reducing the party's ability to persist.[5]

INSTITUTIONALISATION AND DE-INSTITUTIONALISATION

De-institutionalisation can happen not only when the party is fully institutionalised, but also at any time during the process of institutionalisation. Indeed, the effect may then be to slow, halt, or even temporarily reverse that process.

It is an underlying assumption here, however, that while isolated setbacks may happen at any stage of institutionalisation, a full-fledged process of de-institutionalisation is more likely to occur when the organisation is fully institutionalised, when the organisation's leaders are reined in by all that has come before, particularly by the rules and procedures which have been routinised along the way. Indeed, there would seem to be an inverse relationship between institutionalisation and the likelihood that a setback will result in broader institutional decay: to the extent a party is not yet fully institutionalised, setbacks are more likely to be only temporary because leaders/parties have much more flexibility with which to design solutions that can then be implemented more quickly.

Conversely, institutionalisation of routines may actually make the leader's job more difficult when problems arise. The routinisation itself means that there is less room to manoeuvre in designing solutions to the problems. Because of regularisation of leadership selection procedures, it is also more difficult to change a leader mid-term simply because a new problem arises and the current leader is unable or unwilling to respond effectively. And before a strategy can be put into practice, there are more people to be consulted in the institutionalised party, causing not only delay but also the likelihood that the strategy itself will be less coherent, as a reflection of the different interests within the party. If the first leader who faces a problem lacks the wherewithal to solve it and to do so with dispatch, the problem may carry over from one leader to the next, meaning even more time for a disease to take hold and spread.

Nothing above is meant to suggest that fully institutionalised parties are more likely to 'die' compared to younger parties.[6] 'Decay' and 'death' are not synonymous, particularly in that death may certainly occur – and most often does – by means other than decay. Many younger parties die, for instance, simply for lack of popular interest; in most of those cases, institutional decay – or even institutional setbacks – have little or nothing to do with cause of death. By the same token, parties still engaged in the institutionalisation process and facing limited symptoms of decay could – under certain circumstances – avoid lasting negative consequences for reaching full institutionhood.

THE PROGRESS PARTIES AS INSTITUTIONS

In Norway

With the warming of other parties towards the prospects of some day governing with Progress, evidenced first in statements made during the 1989 campaign, the Norwegian Progress Party had taken the final important step from 'new party' to institution. The willingness of the non-socialist minority government to formally negotiate with Hagen over the 1989 budget was a clear sign that the other parties now considered the routinisation of Progress's power in the leader's hands meant that he would be able to keep promises that he made on behalf of his now-institutionalised party.

As if to cast doubt on that point, though, an internal challenge to Hagen's control surfaced in 1994. With growth and with institutionalisation had also come a sub-leadership that was no longer so hand-picked and controllable. As Iversen (1998: 111) notes, the party had by the early 1990s grown to include three identifiable factions: the populists, the value-oriented conservatives, and the ideologically motivated liberalists. The last group – to some extent organised by Hagen himself – would prove to be the most difficult for him to handle. At the 1994 national convention, the liberalists – who controlled the party's youth organisation – pushed for a more consistent liberalistic pro-gramme which included not only the party's traditional economic positions, but also freedom of immigration (i.e. open immigration), which would clearly put the party at odds with its own populists. The liberalists also opposed the important roles attributed to the church and the monarchy, both of which were dear to the party's conservatives. Although Hagen had established a reputation for being able to remain above the factional fray[7], this time he was forced to take sides.

Throwing his lot against the rebellious, young liberalists whom he had recruited and trained, Hagen clearly established that party unity was more important than ideological purity. The liberalists, unable to accept those pri-orities, split from Progress, with four of the ten MPs resigning from the party. The youth organisation dissolved itself, arguing that it was no longer possible to cooperate with the main party.[8] In the end, though, Hagen again prevailed. The power that had by now been routinised in the hands of the leader had allowed Hagen to establish the party's course in the face of disputes within the ranks, and with the most outspoken liberalists gone, the party which Hagen continued to control was actually more coherent than before.

If the 1994 episode had created any new doubt in the minds of other party leaders concerning Hagen's ability to make and deliver on promises for Prog-ress, his handling of that internal challenge should have removed the doubt. And if there were still any doubters concerning his ability to mobilise voters, they should have been convinced by the party's showing in the 1997 Stort-ing election, when the Progress Party won twenty-five seats and became the second-largest group in parliament.[9]

The combination of that strong electoral performance and the weakness of the non-socialist centre government that resulted from the 1997 election[10] placed the Progress Party in a very advantageous position. The government, to remain in office, needed to negotiate with various opposition parties in the

Storting. Having made it a point not to be dependent on one particular ideological wing of the parliament, the government developed a clear negotiating
stance towards the Progress Party. This was seen in particular in the budget
deal for 1998, negotiated between the government on the one side and the
Conservative and Progress parties on the other. Progress was now an 'established player', seen as a party that had to be, *and could be,* reckoned with.

Hagen's attention increasingly turned towards the next election, to be held
in September 2001, and the vision of an even greater role for Progress, now
as a full-fledged governing party. One potential stumbling block, though, still
stood in the way of that objective. The large parliamentary group contained
several controversial MPs, including some with a high anti-immigrant profile.
In the eyes of the party leadership, now placing a premium on Progress's
credibility as a plausible coalition partner, several of these members[11] were
seen as a barrier to that objective.

The effort to make the party 'cabinet acceptable' would involve several
steps. With the ultimate outcome uncertain, the process began in October
2000 when the party's national committee decided that 'it is in the interest
of the party that the leadership trio elected at the national convention should
be represented in parliament in the next period'. The implication of this
decision was to order the relevant province parties – which in all Norwegian
parties control the nomination process – to nominate Carl I. Hagen and his
two deputy chairs, Siv Jensen and Terje Søviknes, at the top of their respective constituency lists.[12] Though there was never any doubt that Hagen would
have been placed at the top of the Oslo list, it is certainly doubtful whether
the local party chair and his allies would have placed Jensen as the second
candidate.

The ensuing conflict over these decisions – and nominations in other constituencies as well – resulted in people being expelled from the party because
of disobeying the decision made by the national committee. Other MPs and
members left in protest over what was seen as an extreme form of centralisation and personal dominance by Carl I. Hagen.[13] The expelled members took
the party to court for violating their rights as party members, with the court
rejecting their case on jurisdictional grounds (as being an internal party matter). When all was said and done, the parliamentary group had been reduced
from twenty-five to twenty, with the high-profile defectors establishing their
own party.

The new party quickly ran into legal problems, as it became unclear what
name the members could run under, and some preferred to run on their own
constituency list. In spite of this, projected electoral support for the mother
party declined during the winter and spring and the press was unanimous in
its verdict that Carl I. Hagen, in his attempt to make the party cabinet acceptable, had achieved exactly the opposite.[14]

Once again, though, the setback was only temporary. During the spring and summer the party's decline levelled off and stabilised with opinion polls showing support at 15 per cent. As the election campaign picked up at the end of the summer holiday, Hagen had once again emerged as a winner in spite of the turmoil.[15] The splinter party/groups were not advancing, and thus offered no real alternative to past Progress supporters. And, in spite of the recent turmoil, the party had not significantly hurt its chances for formal inter-party cooperation sometime in the future.

While remaining in opposition, the Progress Party became Norway's largest non-socialist party upon winning 22.1 per cent of the vote and thirty-eight seats in the 2005 parliamentary election. Hagen handed over the reins to deputy leader Siv Jensen in 2006, who led the party to a record 22.9 per cent of the vote and forty-one parliamentary seats in 2009. At least as important for analysis of institutionalisation, this change of leadership did not result in significant decline of internal party stability. In spite of replacement of the single person whose identity had been so closely intertwined with that of the party for nearly three decades, there were neither defections of representatives nor a decline in membership in the short-term aftermath of the leadership transition. As put by Jupskås (2015: 119):

Figure 8.1 Party leader Carl I. Hagen and Vice-Chair Siv Jensen – who would later succeed Hagen as leader – unveil a portrait of founder Anders Lange on 23 September 2005, as the party took over the room for the second-largest parliamentary group in the Storting. The room had previously been occupied by the Conservative Party. *Credit:* NTB Scanpix; *Photographer:* Erik Johansen.

detailed analyses reveal that the leadership change in 2005/2006 did not cause significant defections. Approximately two thirds of those who were members in 2009 had joined the party before Siv Jensen became leader of the parliamentary party (in 2005) and [of] the extra-parliamentary party (in 2006).

While the latter post-transition behaviour serves as clear evidence of internal value infusion, other evidence – from before the leadership transition – exists to support the conclusion of *external* value infusion as well. In 1987 a poll had shown that 23 per cent of Progress Party voters indicated Carl I. Hagen was the reason for their vote. In 2000 a similar poll found that only 7 per cent indicated Hagen as the reason for their choice (Jupskås 2015: 177–178).

And further evidence of external institutionalisation came in 2013, as the party entered government. Despite winning 'only' 16.3 per cent of the vote in that election, the Progress Party formed a minority coalition government with the Conservative Party, supported by the Liberals and the Christian People's Party.

So, while our analysis through the mid-1990s had led to the conclusion that the Norwegian party was already fully institutionalised, there is nothing in these more recent developments that would cause us to alter that conclusion.

In Denmark

Though Glistrup was officially gone from the party in 1991, that did not mark the end of problems for Kjærsgaard as she continued her attempts to keep the party and its image stabilised. Though the founder had been ousted, several of his long-time supporters remained. With Glistrup gone, some who had been supportive of his earlier claims to being all-powerful now made an issue of the power that Kjærsgaard might wield if not watched carefully. And the two-thirds rule remained a handy tool in the arsenal of those bent on halting her ambitions.

The problems between the Pianists and the former supporters of Glistrup came to a head in the aftermath of what was seen as a less than successful election on 21 September 1994. Taking responsibility, Aage Brusgaard – a Kjærsgaard supporter – resigned as chair of the parliamentary group. On 28 September, the group elected anti-Kjærsgaard candidate Kim Behnke (who had voted against Glistrup's expulsion from the group in 1990) as its chair, by a one-vote margin over Kjærsgaard's preferred candidate. Taking this as a vote of no confidence in her own leadership, Kjærsgaard resigned as spokesperson the next day. On 25 October – while she was away for a month doing party business – the group elected the only official candidate for the spokesperson position, Jan Kopke Christensen.

Factional squabbling would continue for the next year, culminating in the 'party conference from hell' from 30 September to 1 October 1995.[16] With both factions having mobilised grass-roots supporters and having bussed them to the meetings, the stage was set for what would become a nationally televised free-for-all. Exclusions made earlier in the year by the executive committee were now overturned at the national conference. Kjærsgaard supporters on the executive committee whose terms were not yet completed were forced by anti-Kjærsgaard delegates to stand for re-election anyway. Frustrated, humiliated, and embarrassed, Pia Kjærsgaard – followed by three other MPs – resigned from the Progress Party on 6 October 1995, and immediately founded her new alternative, the Danish People's Party (Dansk Folkeparti; DF).

Though there is no denying that the factionalism within the Progress Party had been very personal for many years, the root cause was a fundamental difference over strategy. Kjærsgaard and her supporters felt that policy effectiveness required routinisation of the party's procedures, moderation in its public statements, and a willingness to compromise with other parties: in short, what we have labelled stabilisation! But Glistrup and his supporters had shunned normalisation on virtually all dimensions, favouring an 'all or nothing' approach to policy influence. Now, with Kjærsgaard and most of her supporters gone from the party, and with those supporting Glistrup fully in charge, a stable image for Progress was both devalued and highly unlikely any time in the foreseeable future. As if to confirm rapid deterioration of the party's core electorate, Kjærsgaard's Danish People's Party won 7.5 per cent of the vote and thirteen seats in its first election in 1998, as Progress dropped to 2.4 per cent (from 6.4) and just four seats (from eleven), with subsequent public opinion polls showing similar results.[17] And as evidence of other parties' reactions to the changes in Progress, when Glistrup supporter Kirsten Jacobsen was chosen in 1995 to replace Christensen as spokesperson, the only official leadership position ever held by Glistrup or Kjærsgaard, Conservative Party leader Hans Engell was quoted as saying:

> This is an important political signal. I have so far believed that the party could be included in cooperation and assume political responsibility, but the possibility to become a serious partner in the political game has disappeared with Kirsten Jacobsen's election. ... The Glistrup faction has won a victory. By this [action] the party has left the cooperation line and returned to the pure protest line. (Kjærsgaard 1998: 165–6; authors' translation)

Presumably signalling retraction from any remaining internal value infusion and perhaps putting a nail in their own coffin, from the standpoint of credibility with other parties, Progress welcomed Glistrup back to the party fold in 1999, leading to the split of all remaining party MPs. As a result, the party was required to re-qualify by collecting signatures if it wished to present candidates in the next election. On 30 July 2001, Mogens Glistrup, on behalf of the party, submitted 22,355 signatures to the Interior Ministry for re-registration, with approximately 20,000 required by law (*Politiken* 31 July 2001; Bille 1992: 204). The party won no Folketing seats in the subsequent election and was never re-certified again. Though the party technically continued to exist and survived Glistrup's death in 2008, in reality it lost political relevance – even at the local level – consistently declining in not only local election victories but even in the capacity to nominate candidates.[18]

What had begun with a relatively insubstantial electoral shock (a drop from twelve seats to eleven) had been allowed to escalate into full-blown de-institutionalisation of the party. Routinised procedures were wantonly violated at the 'convention from hell', leading to a critical split at both the elite and electoral levels, coinciding with loss of credibility with other parties, and now the apparent re-personalisation of the party with the founder's triumphal return. Where Hagen and the Norwegian party had succeeded in facing challenges and limiting their negative effects, the Danish party had allowed a challenge to trigger a debilitating process of decay. What explains the difference? Building on earlier chapters, it is reasonable to think that part of the explanation may be found in factors related to party leadership.

DE-INSTITUTIONALISATION AND
LEADERSHIP NEEDS

In chapter 6, we theorised that each phase of development has a distinctive primary objective, coupled with a distinctive set of specific tasks, which in turn corresponds to a distinctive set of leadership needs. In the first phase, the *creator and preacher* is allowed 'maximum freedom' (à la Katz 1973) within which to exercise his or her creativity and communication skills as the party's founder and only visible spokesperson. In the second phase, the *organiser* is already somewhat constrained by his or her own penchant for developing and following organisational routines, as well as delegation of authority to others. In the third phase, the *stabiliser* goes about establishing the party's reputation as credible and dependable by 'maintaining' and 'fine-tuning' what has already been constructed, the job of an 'administrator' rather than a 'grand creator' (i.e. as in the first phase). After reviewing the experiences of the Progress parties in chapter 7, we concluded that the experiences of the two parties had provided support for those expectations.

All that has gone before leads us now to ask the question: What type of 'special skills', if any, might be required of political parties (or more specifically, the entrepreneurial issue parties) once they have reached 'institution-hood'? An answer to that question is required if we are to take the theory of 'party development and changing leadership needs' one step further, that is, to include the period which begins immediately after the party becomes fully institutionalised.

At first blush, it may seem that what is needed most is a leader who is adept at simply maintaining the status quo. But even if 'maintaining the status quo' were the goal, the word 'simply' would be missing the mark by a wide margin.

As noted above, the fact that a party is fully institutionalised does not preclude significant challenges to the party's stability, some of which may directly or indirectly lead to de-institutionalisation on one or more dimensions. Changes in the electorate or the party system may result in significant electoral downturns; struggles among contending factions may fuel internal turmoil; scandals or ill-judged positions may shake the confidence of other parties – those are but a few examples of the perils that might still befall even the fully institutionalised party.

It is not the frequency of such 'problems' that distinguishes the institutionalising party from the party that is fully institutionalised (unless, of course, unbridled decay sets in). Rather it is the extent to which, and the ways in which, leaders are constrained in their ability to develop and implement solutions. Where the 'creator and preacher' of the first phase worked nearly alone and hence with maximum freedom, where the 'organiser' would develop the organisational controls that would rein in future leaders, and where the 'stabiliser' was already maintaining and fine-tuning what had been created earlier, the leader of the fully institutionalised party must function as a stabiliser – a maintainer and *problem-solver* working within a limiting, institutionalised set of rules, procedures, traditions, and expectations.

As such, the problem-solver must be capable of working within organisational routines, but also be skilled in working with others to revise those routines as necessary. This leader must also be willing and able to use whatever power is available within those routines, especially when quick and dramatic change is necessary. Relatedly, while the problem-solver of the institutionalised party must be willing to work within a routinised system, he/she must not be opposed to change, per se. (By the same token, though, this should not be someone who is easily bored – and hence prone to change for the sake of change – when no change is required.) This person would benefit from being a 'student' of the party and of politics generally, an asset in picking up signs of impending problems. For the same purpose, this leader should be a good 'listener' (in contrast to the skilled 'communicator' of the first phase), keeping in regular contact with other relevant players.

As we argued above, a fully institutionalised party may be more prone to multidimensional decay than are younger parties, simply because of the greater limitations upon leaders in the institutionalised party. For this reason, the problem-solver of the institutionalised party must be willing to do what it takes to stop decay as soon as it is recognised. What may be required is a surgeon who is willing and able to cut away the decaying portion in order to save the rest of the body, for instance, when it becomes necessary to eject a faction bent on flouting normal organisational procedures.

Armed with this rather complex job description, we now turn to examining the Progress parties during their early years of middle age.

Application to the Progress Parties since the Mid-1990s

Having already established that the Danish party has de-institutionalised and the Norwegian party has not, it remains for us to consider the role that leadership may have played in the differing experiences of these two parties.

In the Norwegian case, Hagen – who was nothing if not a student of party organisation and politics – had at times been problem-maker as well as problem-solver. Adopting positions which drew public scorn to his party, for instance, he was generally able to then restore a semblance of moderacy and stability before long-term damage could be done. The net result: valuable public attention being paid to the party and its agenda at crucial times!

In 2001, when the populist faction refused to accept what it perceived to be the national committee's interference in the nomination process, the surgeon Hagen showed his willingness to take scalpel in hand and remove what he saw as hindering the party's chances for participation in government. Some in the uncooperative faction were expelled and others left in protest. That the party – after a brief decline coinciding with the turmoil – stabilised its position in both opinion polls and electoral support would be taken as a sign that the surgery was done skillfully and successfully. The setback that some had feared did not materialise, with Hagen being the recipient of much of the credit.

Post-Hagen – who stepped away from leadership in 2005/2006 – his replacement Siv Jensen appeared to have the problem-solving skills necessary to both maintain unity within the party and negotiate government cooperation with multiple other parties.

In the Danish party, Kjærsgaard's departure in 1995, coming on the heels of the 'convention from hell' at which her 'normal party' candidates for party offices had been defeated, effectively left the party in the hands of Glistrup supporters. If those events were the ultimate signs of Kjærsgaard's own inability to play the problem-solver role, there was no evidence that the subsequent leadership could do any better. Though it is true that the party was significantly reduced in size by the split, it is also true that what remained was more coherent and consequently more prone to leadership. And still, the party continued to decline. The decision to bring Glistrup and his anti-normal ways and reputation back into the party may have been the most significant leadership failure of all, effectively sealing the party's fate and failing to solve any of the critical problems reflected in the events of 1995.

The differing experiences of the two parties may seem, at first glance, to suggest a difference in the problem-solving abilities of Hagen and the leaders who followed Kjærsgaard; and even of Hagen and Kjærsgaard – who was, after all, the leader during the onset of the Danish party's crisis of decay. But we would be seriously remiss to end this study with that impression alone. Such a conclusion would ignore not only the evidence that Kjærsgaard had already demonstrated problem-solving skills both as organiser and stabiliser, but also that Hagen had a clear organisational advantage.

Though it is true that both parties had become fully institutionalised, with all that means for routinisation of controls, there is still substantial room for variation in leaders' manoeuvrability. As important as institutionalisation itself, and perhaps even more so, is *what* has been institutionalised. And that 'what' was very different between the two Progress parties. Hagen had assumed leadership at a low point for his party, to fill what had effectively been a leadership vacuum. In that context, he led the routinisation of very strong, central leadership, with one individual capable of steering and imposing an aura of coherence even to a party with undeniably competing tendencies. Kjærsgaard, on the other hand, assumed effective leadership with an 'other leader' remaining constantly in the picture. Glistrup's presence would be felt even while in prison, and when he returned to his lifetime position on the main board his followership within the party was largely intact. In such an environment, what became institutionalised was centralised but divided leadership, reflecting both the initial interest in concentrating power in a main board which Glistrup's personality would presumably dominate, coupled with the reality that in later years the main board was itself deeply divided between Glistrup supporters and Kjærsgaard's reformists. Adding to Kjærsgaard's difficulties in consolidating control was the tradition (not a 'rule', but routinised nonetheless) against simultaneously being a member of parliament and leader of the extra-parliamentary party; Hagen did not share that problem.

CONCLUSION

In earlier chapters, we described and attempted to explain the process of institutionalisation within the two Progress parties. In the process, we developed a theory of 'party development and leadership needs', in which we argued that particular leadership orientations and skills are required at each of three phases of institutionalisation, and that turmoil will result for the party which fails to meet the needs in each phase. In this chapter, we have extended the development-and-needs theory to help understand the differing experiences of the two parties in the early years of post-institutionalisation.

There is nothing in those experiences that contradicts the notion that institutionalised entrepreneurial issue parties require the orientations and skills of a 'problem-solver' to successfully isolate instances of de-institutionalisation. In Norway, where Hagen had both the orientations and the skills, challenges were met and long-term decay was avoided. In Denmark, though, where Kjærsgaard may have had many of the requisite skills, she reacted to early signs of decay by resigning – first from her leadership position and then from the party – and thus participated in the party's decomposition rather than its salvation. While some might attribute this to a weakness in Kjærsgaard's character, as compared to that of Hagen, we subscribe to a different view. Kjærsgaard's final actions may well have resulted from rationally calculating the improbability of leading this particular party back to normalcy, given how difficult it had been to lead it even in what had passed as 'normal' times.

While the skills of the problem-solver may be *necessary* in order to fend off decay, they may not be *sufficient*. Though institutionalisation always results in greater constraints on party leaders, *what* has been institutionalised is also critical. When what has been institutionalised is divided leadership plus acute factionalism, as in the Danish party, it may be impossible for any leader to devise and implement a strategy for reversing a serious onset of decay. When, on the other hand, routinisation has put substantial control and flexibility in the hands of the leader, as in the Norwegian party, it is more reasonable to expect an appropriately skilled leader to solve problems as they arise, and hence avoid long-term decay.

In sum: for the institutionalised party, when it comes to isolating instances of decay and avoiding acute decomposition, leadership matters! But leadership depends on more than just traits; it also requires a receptive institution.

NOTES

1. Such practices continued for subsequent non-socialist governments in both countries, though the Danish party would never be invited into government. The closest that party came was in advance of the 1994 election when other parties seriously considered going into government with Progress. Election results, though, rendered that impossible. In 2013, the Norwegian party did enter into a minority government with the Conservatives, supported by the Liberal and Christian People's parties.

2. Here we clearly differ with Oliver (1992), who focuses at the micro level and treats change from one routinised practice or activity to another as de-institutionalisation. 'Replacement' is thus explicitly considered by Oliver to be a form of de-institutionalisation, along with dissipation or rejection.

3. For instance, some observers of the British Labour Party speculated that late-comers to party membership who joined because of their support for Jeremy Corbyn as party leader might exit the party if/when Corbyn was replaced.

4. In the Danish Progress Party, founder Mogens Glistrup's period in prison was met with a strengthening of the party under new leadership in the parliamentary wing. In Norway, the Progress Party lost its founder in its first year; after a few years of unsuccessful replacements, the party elected the pro-organisation and very successful Carl I. Hagen as its leader.

5. While we ourselves are particularly interested in the institutionalisation and de-institutionalisation of *entrepreneurial issue parties*, which share with other char-ismatic or pseudo-charismatic parties their origins as creations and creatures of their founding leaders, there is no reason why application of the conceptual framework presented here should be limited to such parties. The dimensions of external insti-tutionalisation and objective durability – and their reversals – are fully applicable to any party. And the primary feature of the 'routinisation' dimension is not transforma-tion from a *charismatic party*, per se, but rather the replacement of ad hoc decision-making by routinised behaviour patterns.

6. Indeed, research on life expectancies of organisations generally supports the conclusion that organisations are more likely to die young than old (see, for instance, Bolleyer 2013; Stinchcombe 1965; Whetten 1980).

7. According to Iversen (1998: 128), Hagen could be characterised as economi-cally liberalistic, conservative in values, and populistic in form.

8. The youth organisation was immediately re-established by the Progress Party itself.

9. During the next three years, the party experienced increasing support in opinion polls, reaching 34.3 per cent in September 2000 (*Aftenposten* 15 September 2000). In public sentiment, the Progress Party thus became the largest party in Nor-way, relegating Labour to second place.

10. The Labour government resigned, it said, because it had not won as large a share of the votes as it felt it needed (i.e. 36.9 per cent) to continue in office. This resignation opened the way for a non-socialist government, consisting of the Christian People's Party, the Liberals and the Centre Party. The government had just 25 per cent of the seats in parliament behind it.

11. Popularly known as '*verstinger*' (the worst ones).

12. Carl I. Hagen and Siv Jensen would represent the Oslo constituency; Søviknes was to be nominated in Hordaland constituency in western Norway.

13. In an attempt to rally the parliamentary group behind Carl I. Hagen a declara-tion was adopted praising him for his leadership: 'The party chairman is a strong and dynamic leader demanding a lot from his colleagues and even more demanding with regard to his own efforts. The members of the [party] group strongly reject claims that Hagen's style of leadership is reason for resigning from the party and the group' (*Verdens Gang* 8 February 2001).

14. By coincidence, the party at this point became embroiled in a scandal as the deputy chair was accused of sexual misconduct against a young female party member at a party meeting. The deputy chair was forced to resign from the position and temporarily resigned from his position as mayor in a municipality when under

investigation by the police for possible criminal acts. A related incident involving another party office holder also surfaced at this time (Hagen 2007: 381–90).

15. It should be noted that Hagen's popularity among the electorate in general may have suffered, at least temporarily, as a result of the party turmoil. When the party's national convention met at the end of April 2001, a majority of the voters surveyed (54 per cent) answered that they had a more negative impression of him than compared to a year earlier. However, inside the party, Hagen seemed as much in control as ever: the previous months of turmoil were barely mentioned and hardly anyone challenged the proposal for the new party programme (*Bergens Tidende* 28 April 2001; *Aftenposten* 28 April 2001). Olav Kobbeltvedt, a journalist, reported from the Progress Party convention for the *Bergens Tidende* (28 April 2001) that 'there was more opposition at the congresses of the Communist parties in the time of Stalin'.

16. A significant amount of the detail in this and the following paragraph comes from 'The Development of the Danish Progress Party', a term paper produced by Sophie Haestorp Andersen for a Spring 1999 graduate seminar at the University of Copenhagen, with Robert Harmel and Lars Bille as instructors. Andersen, in turn, drew much of the information from Pedersen (1997) and Kjærsgaard (1998).

17. The electoral success of the Danish People's Party continued in the 2001 election, winning 12 per cent of the vote and twenty-two parliamentary seats. The electoral support remained stable in subsequent elections, and in 2011 the party won 12.3 per cent of the vote and twenty-two seats, retaining its position as Denmark's third largest party since 2001. Pia Kjærsgaard remained leader until 2012, when she voluntarily stepped down and parliamentary leader Kristian Thulesen Dahl left that post and assumed the position of party leader.

18. From nominating 1028 candidates for municipal councils and winning 133 seats in 1993 (prior to the split), the party had declined to nominating only 268 candidates and winning just 5 seats in 2001. (http://www.statistikbanken.dk/statbank5a/default.asp?w=1745 Accessed 14 January 2017). Although the party may have continued to nominate candidates in some localities, the numbers were so small that the party ceased to be listed in the regularly published statistics.

Part IV

CONCLUSIONS

Chapter 9

Conclusions

It has been our purpose in this book to contribute to knowledge on how parties institutionalise, why some are successful in doing so in spite of heavy odds against them, and why some – having fully institutionalised – reverse the process, de-institutionalise, and ultimately disappear from the political scene. In pursuing that purpose, we have told significant parts of the stories of two 'new' parties of the 1970s, one each in Denmark and Norway, neither of which could have been expected to reach full institutionhood. That both did so, and that one continues to this day while the other decayed and died, have presented the interesting 'puzzles' to which we have attempted to offer plausible solutions.

In the process, we have suggested a number of factors which we feel contributed to the institutionalisation of these parties, in spite of having a number of characteristics which theoretically should have made institutionalisation difficult if not impossible. Born into the class of 'right-wing protest parties', neither the Danish nor the Norwegian Progress parties faced an easy path to institutionhood. Indeed, at the time of their births, in the early 1970s, political scientists would have been among those predicting a difficult road ahead for both parties. These were, after all, parties which appeared to fit the designations 'charismatic' and 'protest'-focused, and with more of a 'movement' than a 'party' organisational style, any one of which could have doomed the parties to early demise. Indeed, the 'protest' in both cases was against deeply engrained values associated with the social democratic systems and cultures of the two host countries, something which would hardly seem to smooth the difficulties.

Throughout chapters 5 and 7, we have identified a number of factors which seemingly did contribute to these parties' institutionalisation. Any attempt to generalise from these cases – that is to amend extant theory with

131

circumstances which may improve such parties' chances for institutionalisation – should take these factors into account:

1. Though parties of the 'hard charismatic' variety may indeed find it difficult if not impossible to reify so as to endure beyond departure of the founder, parties of the 'entrepreneurial issue' type are identified with their positions in addition to the personality of the leader, giving them an advantage on the path towards institutionalisation. The latter is true even given that the original 'preacher' of the message may have been critical to the *beginning* of the party.[1]
2. Though parties founded by leaders favouring more of a movement-style organisation may indeed suffer schisms over strategy, between those wanting to continue a movement style and those preferring the organisational approach of other parties, such schisms may be avoided or at least diminished according to the extent that the 'movement' was initially developed to provide support for a new party rather than long before any party formation.
3. Though parties whose only message is negative 'protest' may indeed find it difficult to sustain support in the absence of electoral successes, more enduring support may be found by protest parties which quickly develop more positive approaches to governing and/or whose message directly addresses deeply held societal values in such a way as to strike an especially responsive chord for an important segment of the electorate.

Not only were both Progress parties 'entrepreneurial issue parties' which developed simultaneously with their founders 'movements' and offered messages which engendered sustained interest, but both also developed the 'right leaders for the time' for each of the critical stages on the way to institutionalisation. Glistrup and Lange met the requirements for 'preaching' in the first stage, and both departed in time for replacement by those more qualified to pursue development of party organisation and stabilisation. Parties whose early preachers failed to give way to successors with skills and temperament for the later stages would certainly be more likely to falter and fail to achieve institutionhood.

In recounting that the Progress parties benefited from all of these 'special circumstances', we would certainly be remiss not to recognise the roles played by 'timing' and sheer 'luck' in the provision of those and other circumstances which aided their institutionalisation. Had Lange not passed away and had Glistrup not gone to prison in the early years of their parties, it is unlikely that the likes of Hagen and Kjærsgaard would have had the opportunity to play their critical roles in development of 'normal organisation' and stabilising images. Were it not for development of younger generations of Danes and Norwegians who were quite willing to question the values and premises underlying the political and social status quo, there would not have been such a receptive audience for the Progress parties' messages of protest and change.

There are other reasons too why the Danish and Norwegian political contexts of the 1970s may have been more welcoming – or at least supportive – of new parties like Progress at the time of their formation and then institutionalisation. For instance, public subsidies for parties with parliamentary representation were introduced in Norway in 1970, just a few years before the birth of Progress. Though the subsidies certainly did not 'cause' the development of Progress, the availability of public funds would undoubtedly have provided important financial support for the party in its earliest years of existence. Though direct public subsidies were not yet available to all parties in Denmark, the system provided other important infrastructure – including office space and staff support – for new parties (as well as older parties) with representation in parliament.[2] Such parties would also have been aided by the fact that television (with equal 'free' treatment for all parties) and other non-partisan media were in the process of replacing party-connected newspapers as the vehicles of choice for obtaining political information.

In pointing to these 'special' advantages enjoyed by the two Progress parties, we certainly do not mean to suggest that they are or were uniquely advantaged among parties of their ilk worldwide. To the contrary, we see each of these particular circumstances – with the possible exceptions of 'timing' and 'good fortune' – as factors which may be present in other right-wing protest parties elsewhere. Rather than positioning our two parties as 'unique', these circumstances should instead be seen as the types of factors which may distinguish between parties of the same type which 'flash in the pan' and those which successfully defy the presumed odds and institutionalise.

Indeed, we have not been alone in identifying and analysing instances of 'new' right-wing parties which have faced similar challenges on the path to institutionhood. The emergence of the Progress parties in the 1970s was followed by a number of new party formations in European democracies, some of which shared the characteristics of the Progress parties as being formed by entrepreneurs, being on the right and, at least initially, seeing themselves and being seen by others as protest parties (Poguntke 1996; Schedler 1996). A few of these parties have been labelled examples of successful institutionalisation. Arter and Kestilla-Kekkonen (2014) concluded that the True Finns in Finland had institutionalised, according to their operationalisation of the concept. And of course, Berlusconi's Forza Italia has by many accounts been the most successful of the modern entrepreneurial parties, having remained a pivotal party in a large country for a considerable period of time. And others – for example, New Democracy in Sweden and List Pim Fortuyn in the Netherlands – fulfilled expectations and died young and uninstitutionalised;

the number of such parties is uncertain, since poor if any records are kept of many new party formations which die, quite literally, 'without a trace'.

Though it is well beyond the scope of this book to systematically compare these other successes and failures among parties sharing features of the Progress parties (though it should be the purpose of another book), it is possible to highlight a few similarities and differences between these other cases and our own[3]. Of the parties which failed to institutionalise, structural problems related to leadership were certainly a factor in the demise of New Democracy, List Pym Fortuyn, and the earlier case of the Poujadists in France.[4] In the Swedish case, the party imploded when the original leader suddenly decided to leave the party and no established routines were in place to handle the leadership transition (Svåsand and Wørlund 2001). In the end, the party went bankrupt and disappeared from the political scene. Lack of a developed organisational base was also instrumental in the collapse of the List Pym Fortuyn. According to de Lange and Art (2011), lack of routinised procedures for handling differences involving candidates and activists led to open conflicts and ultimate party failure upon the assassination of the party's leader and namesake. 'Timing' was also a critical factor, with electoral success coming before the party had time to develop effective organisation.[5] In France, Poujade was recognised as leader of both a *movement* and the Poujadist *party*, and though they existed simultaneously, he made no effort to join the two or, for that matter, to develop any extra-parliamentary organisation for the party. After an initial electoral success (winning fifty-two seats in the National Assembly in 1956), Poujade defected from his own namesake party, which essentially disintegrated prior to the next election.

So far in this chapter, we have spoken only of particular factors contributing to the *institutionalisation* of a privileged subset of right-wing protest parties. We cannot conclude this book without touching again upon the topic of chapter 8, the *de-institutionalisation* of such parties even after reaching full institutionhood. The Danish Progress Party provided us with the opportunity to explore both institutionalisation and de-institutionalisation, within the twenty-nine-year lifespan of a single party. Because our other party – the counterpart in Norway – has not experienced de-institutionalisation even at the time of writing, we have no reason to conclude the inevitability of either post-institutionalisation success or failure for such parties. To the contrary, these two parties' post-1995 experiences have provided us with the necessary underpinnings for informed speculation on factors which separate long-term from temporary institutionhood.

Of all the factors we have identified in the institutionalisation of right-wing protest parties, we have considered the meeting of stage-related leadership needs to be most critical. While other special circumstances aided the Progress parties on the path to institutionalisation, it would not have been possible without the timely replacement of the party founders. But as we have argued in chapter 8, fully institutionalised parties also have special leadership needs which, if left unmet, may contribute to institutional decay.

Though the True Finns and Forza Italia have been identified as cases elsewhere in Europe which have institutionalised, there is scepticism concerning their abilities to remain so. And here, the lessons learned from study of the Progress parties – and especially the de-institutionalisation of the Danish party – could certainly be germane. In finding the True Finns to have institutionalised, Arter and Kestilla-Kekkonen (2014) include this cautionary statement concerning the party's future: '*de-institutionalisation* can be sudden and swift' (952). Among the sources for concern is that the party had not – as of the time of their writing – experienced any leadership succession at the top (953). While the Forza Italia may be the most 'successful' of these parties to date, lack of routinisation and de-personalisation could also prove to be problematic. Though considered by many to be 'institutionalised', the party is nevertheless completely dominated by the party leader in terms of important functions, such as candidate nominations, finances, and internal communication. McDonnell (2013) found that among senior party elites at the time of his study, a majority doubted that the party could survive Berlusconi's departure.[6]

It has been the underlying premise of this book that all of the above parties – certainly including the two parties whose stories we have told in some detail – are of a type that face special challenges to avoid being just a 'flash in the pan'. While becoming 'institutions' is certainly no easy task for any new party, right-wing protest parties of entrepreneurial origins face a number of special hurdles on the way to institutionhood. And for those which reach that status, remaining there has its own challenges – at least some of which were engrained at their origins. It has been our primary purpose to further the development of theory to aid in understanding why it is that some such parties – in spite of the presumed odds against it – do succeed in achieving institution status, and then why it is that some keep it while others lose it. Analysis of the experiences of the Norwegian and Danish Progress parties, as told here in some detail, has yielded the lesson that – while other factors are important as well – having the right leader at the right time is critical both for gaining institutionhood *and for keeping it*. From the experiences of these parties and others (some of which have been briefly treated above), it appears that similar parties will ignore this lesson at their peril.

NOTES

1. This distinction is more relevant when comparing Western European entrepreneurial parties to the 'entrepreneurial person' parties of less-developed democracies.

2. Since 1965, the parliamentary parties have been supported to hire consultants and expert assistance, with grants proportional to the parties' share of seats. Though the funds were originally intended just for parliamentary group support, 'in real terms the grant was a supplement to party finances taken as a whole' (Bille 1994: 146). A law granting state subvention to party organisations as such was passed in 1986 and implemented in 1987.

3. See the appendix for a summary of research findings on parties similar to the two Progress parties.

4. The same could be said for the centre-left Italy of Values party, which Pasquino (2014: 558) characterises as 'a group of politically ambitious individuals running for and holding office'. The party's dominant leader for virtually all of its fifteen years of existence had no interest in developing party organisation on the ground.

5. In contrast, the successor party to LPF, the PVV – the party led by Geert Wilders – successfully institutionalised. Wilder's PVV was built from the ground up, prior to its national electoral breakthrough. Wilders had learned from the mistakes of the LPF and had invested in building a party culture (see de Lange and Art 2011).

6. Another party which parallels the rise and fall of the Danish Progress Party to some degree is the Rural Party in Finland. Formed in 1958 as the Finnish Smallholders Party, the party leader had been a member of the Agrarian Party, and as such did not emerge from outside the political arena as Glistrup had done. The party, renamed the Rural Party in 1966, had its breakthrough election in 1970 with 10 per cent of the votes. The transition of the leadership from the original founder to his son was the start of the decline. Although so successful that it became part of the government between 1983 and 1990, long before similar parties would be included among the established parties in other Scandinavian countries, the leadership transition and governmental participation ushered in conflicts between factions and triggered defections from the party. In 1995 the party had only one seat in the Finnish parliament, after which it folded (Widtfeldt 2000). In that same year, the True Finns (later aka The Finns) were founded on essentially the same platform.

Appendix

Comparative Cases

Three distinguishing characteristics of the Progress parties are: 1) they were formed as *entrepreneurial parties*; 2) they were (and are) *right-wing* parties; and 3) they were seen, initially, and saw themselves, as *protest parties*. There are several European political parties, historical as well as contemporary, that are frequently seen as similar to the Progress parties, but which do not necessarily share all of these characteristics of those two parties. The purpose of this appendix is to describe some of these comparative cases, and in the process to identify both similarities and differences, as well as special characteristics and roles of leaders. We should begin by making clear that while we see this as an illustrative set of cases, it is not intended to be either an exhaustive or a random sample of such parties. Instead this is more of a convenience sample, in that it is limited to parties that have gained sufficient academic attention to be covered in extant literature.

Before briefly describing each of the parties, we will first highlight how some of them deviate from one or two of the Progress parties' defining characteristics as entrepreneurial right-wing protest parties. The first variant concerns the type of individual leadership that triggered the formation of the parties. The Progress parties were formed as *entrepreneurial* parties, which are a subset of a larger group of parties – 'personal parties' – in which the party leader dominates the way the party functions (Kostadinova and Levitt 2014). We reserve the term 'entrepreneurial' for parties formed by *outsiders,* in the sense that they hold no elective public office. All of the parties we describe below have been created by individual actors, but not all were created by outsider entrepreneurs. For example, the Dutch PVV – formed by an individual, but in this case a political *insider* – is not an *entrepreneurial* party in our conception. It nonetheless deserves to be included in the broader category of 'personal' parties. The distinction between the two sub-categories – entrepreneurial and insider personal parties – may be important for institutionalisation as the latter type of parties can draw on expertise and networks that the former type likely does without. It is an empirical question – and one worthy of more systematic study elsewhere – whether the two types of leader-dependent parties actually differ in terms of institutionalisation. For now, it seems noteworthy that the one example of an *insider* personal party included in our small sample – the PVV – was founded by an insider with a penchant for a *very non-traditional* organisational style, and hence it is one that may not in fact have the advantages for institutionalisation that other such parties might possess.

The second variable dimension is the parties' ideological location and issue profile. The Progress parties were definitely on the *right* when they were founded, and initially both were primarily concerned with taxation. Some of the cases below deviate from the Progress parties on the ideological dimension. For instance, the Italian Party of Values was entrepreneurial, but not on the right.

Finally, many new parties are seen as *protest* parties. However, not all entrepreneurial or internal personal parties are protest parties concerned with the same issues as the Progress parties. Beppe Grillo's Five Star Movement is an entrepreneurial party and may be seen as a protest party, but in this case the protest is against the whole structure of the Italian political system. The Five Star Movement is not easily located on the right, and refuses to see itself as part of the left-right dimension. Berlusconi's Forza Italia is not a protest party, but is both right-wing and entrepreneurial.

Thus, parties that are often seen as 'similar' to the Progress parties are not necessarily like the Progress parties on all key characteristics.

The group of parties described below covers a variety of historical, political, and technological contexts. This means that the internal factors that influence institutionalisation processes and/or the environments of the parties may be different from those of the Progress parties. The treatment of these parties is based on existing literature, not on our own primary research. We do not claim to be covering all parties that could be called entrepreneurial or personal parties, but we do believe there is enough variation among these parties that taken together, the cases below may shed light on the generalizability of the findings concerning the institutionalisation of the Progress parties. Because we rely on existing research, it is inevitable that there are variations in how much information about our dimensions of institutionalisation there is for each of the individual parties.

All of the parties below are what have been called 'personalistic' (or 'personal') parties in the broader sense discussed above.[1,2,3] Two of the parties – the Swiss Lega dei Ticinesi (LT) and the Dutch Party of Freedom (PVV) – are completely leadership-dependent, though they nonetheless are substantially different from all the other cases, even on this dimension. These are what Mazzoleni and Voerman (2017) call '*memberless* parties'. They constitute a special category because they *make no attempt* to build any form of party *organisation* as it is usually understood in the literature. These are nonetheless interesting cases, because at least one of them – the LT – comes close to having become institutionalised, while it is less clear that the other case has done or will do so. We begin with these parties, and then move to those with more 'normal' organisational orientations.

MEMBERLESS PARTIES

Mazzoleni and Voerman (2017) have analysed the development of the Dutch Party of Freedom (PVV) and the Swiss Lega dei Ticinesi (LT). These are parties where there is no attempt to construct anything like a regular party organisation with a hierarchical structure, members, and organisational units. Our framework includes the dimension *organisational routinisation* that is clearly absent from this type of party.

Italy: Lega dei Ticinesi (LT)

The LT (a sub-national party in the canton of Ticino) is an *entrepreneurial* party, formed by Giuliano Bignasca – a successful businessman – in 1991. It was deliberately constructed so that the party leader is the only party member. LT emphasizes its 'protest against the Swiss government, with its large and durable party coalitions' (Mazzoleni and Voerman 2017: 788). Immigration and EU-scepticism have been added to its agenda. The entrepreneurial origin and the protest orientation make the party similar to the Progress parties, though the 'protest' in this case was, at least initially, directed against the Swiss system of governing.

In lieu of a 'standard' party organisation, the party's elected representatives constitute an informal committee. The party's so-called highest organ, the constitutional assembly, has never met. The party has managed to survive the death of its party founder in 2013. However, the 'transition' to a *new* leadership can perhaps be called 'partial', as the new leader is the brother of the party founder. This means that all the resources needed for running the party remain within the family of the party's founder. Hence the party has avoided routinisation of normal party organisation up to this point.

In the case of LT there is obviously no internal value infusion among members, since there is only one member. Nevertheless, the party has achieved external recognition at the cantonal level. It currently holds two of the five seats in the cantonal government of Ticino and it is the largest party in the cantonal parliament (Mueller and Mazzoleni 2016).

LT has achieved objective durability as the party has existed for twenty-five years and it has survived the death of the original party founder. Given its proven durability in combination with its role in cantonal government, it seems reasonable to assert that the party has achieved external institutionalisation in the eyes of other cantonal parties. So, the experience of LT seems to establish that it is possible for a party which lacks any form of internal institutionalisation to still achieve some form of external institutionalisation and experience objective durability.

Netherlands: Party of Freedom (PVV)

Another 'memberless' party is the right-wing, anti-immigrant Party of Freedom (PVV) in the Netherlands, founded in 2005/2006 by Geert Wilders, who had served as a member of parliament for the Liberal Party from 1998 until 2004. Before that he had been a professional staff person in parliament. According to Vossen, 'few Dutch politicians can boast a more thorough knowledge of all parliamentary procedures, conventions and informal networks with the Parliament' (2010: 29). Because of Wilders' status as an insider at the time of his founding of the new party, PVV is not an entrepreneurial party like the Progress parties, but is instead an *insider personal party*.

This party cannot be considered routinised for one simple reason: like the LT, it has only one member – the founder Wilders himself![4] Although the PVV won nine seats in parliament in the 2006 election, these representatives are not *members* of the PVV in the normal sense for European parties. And as candidates running for office, they were handpicked by Wilders. Indeed, formally, the PVV has no party organisational structure. In practical terms it does appear to function much like other parties: it has MPs and local representatives, people maintaining the website, and volunteers campaigning for the party; it nominates candidates, runs election campaigns, and has party fractions in the two houses of the Dutch parliament. But all of the 'functions' as a party are *decided* by the party leader, Geert Wilders, himself.[5] The statutes even leave it to Wilders to appoint his successor; this includes the power to revoke the appointment.

Though loyalty within the parliamentary group is quite strong (de Lange and Art 2011: 1237), it is unclear if the target of loyalty is the party leader or the party and its political programme. And precisely because of Wilders' dominant position, there have been several conflicts, and new representatives of the party seem less willing to be sidelined. According to Akkerman, 'internal organization is the principal problem the party faces' (2016: 164). At best, it seems premature to assert that value infusion has been accomplished among public office holders. And, as with the LT, it would seem ludicrous to argue that party value has been infused in the one party member.

On the other hand, the PVV has achieved a form of external recognition, having forged a formal agreement with the government to vote in favour of most of its proposals and to support it in case the opposition proposes a vote of no confidence (de Lange and Art 2011: 1235). But in the absence of other relevant information, and given that the party has not been considered for participation in government, it is not possible to conclude whether the party has accomplished external institutionalisation in the eyes of other parties.

In spite of de Lange and Art's claim that the PVV has institutionalised (de Lange and Art 2011), one can argue that the crucial test of institutionalisation will come when Wilders is no longer the party leader. De Lange and Art cite several of the PVV's parliamentarians who praise Wilders' leadership qualities. It is clear, however, that he has not seen fit to use those qualities to build anything approaching normal party organisation. And it cannot be assumed that party representatives in the future will accept his dominant position; and in any case, leadership qualities are not necessarily transferable. In the absence of any leadership transition, survivability is not ensured. Hence, while 'the report card is still out' on a number of dimensions, it would seem that a pronouncement of institutionhood for the PVV is premature at best, and is far from assured.

The remaining cases described below include three examples of *failed* entrepreneurial parties: the Poujade movement in France (1953–58), the Swedish New Democracy (1991–95), and the Italian Party of Values (1998–2013). Two other parties, the Five Star Party (MS5) and Berlusconi's Forza Italia (and its permutations), are not yet fully institutionalised, but *continue to exist* at the time of writing.

PARTIES THAT FAILED TO INSTITUTIONALISE

France: The Poujadists (UFF)

The Poujadist movement in 1950s France provides an interesting parallel – and contrast – to the rise of the Progress parties in Norway and Denmark in the 1970s. There are several similarities with regard to the leadership and the issues, but the contrast is the short life of the Poujade movement.

Post-war France's Fourth Republic had a very fragmented party system with multiple political movements and parties.[6] One of these, UDCA (Union de defense des commercants et des artisans), was formed in 1953 by political outsider Pierre Poujade. The movement mobilised strong support from groups of voters who perceived that they were suffering under economic reforms and who felt alienated from the mainstream political parties and the

institutions of the Republic. It is common therefore to characterise the Poujade movement as a right-wing protest movement.

There are several similarities with the early years of the Progress parties. First, the UDCA movement was very much identified with its founder.
And, again like the Progress parties, it focused on taxation issues, which in
the movement's view hurt ordinary shop owners and artisans in particular.
Initially, the movement did not aspire to form a political party, but in 1955
it established the organisation UFF (Union et fraternite Francaise) to launch
candidates for the 1956 parliamentary elections, after having concluded that
in order to have an impact on the political system it was necessary to be represented in the National Assembly (Fitzgerald 1970: 177). To its own – and
to its competitors' – surprise, it polled more than two million votes and won
fifty-two seats for its representatives, few of whom had any political experience (Williams 1972: 164).

But the group's impact on politics in parliament seems to have been nil
(Shields: 2004), and like the early Progress party parliamentary groups, the
Poujadists were shunned by the other parties. According to Williams, they
'were rarely courted by and never made any impression upon their colleagues' (Williams 1972: 165). Adding to this marginalisation was the fact
that the UFF did not have any blackmail potential, in that its support was not
needed for coalition building.

There were also internal problems in the parliamentary group that contributed to its undoing. In spite of attempts by Poujade to exercise discipline
in the group, there were multiple cases of members defying the party line
on crucial votes.[7] The group was quickly reduced as eleven of its members
were expelled for violating the campaign finance regulations, and defections
reduced the group to thirty (Shields 2004: 40). By 1958, two years after its
electoral success, Poujade broke with his own party group.[8] Some of the
UFF MPs left to join the Independents in parliament, while twenty-two MPs
formed a new 'anti-tax' group, UALS (Groupe d'union et d'action liberale
et socials) (Marcum 1959: 172). As the political chaos of the Fourth Republic continued, the majority of the MPs elected for the Poujadists ended up
approving de Gaulle as the new prime minister as well as voting for his new
constitution.[9] In the following election the party lost all of its seats and finally
disappeared from the political landscape together with the Fourth Republic
itself. Even Poujade asked his supporters to vote for the Gaullist party in the
last election of the Fourth Republic in 1958 (Williams 1970: 280).

In spite of the similarities with the Progress parties – having an entrepreneurial leadership, the early electoral breakthrough, the focus on taxes,
and the anti-establishment character – there were also some differences
regarding the internal organisation. While the leaders of the Progress parties
were dominant figures able to retain control of their parties, the Poujadist

movement ultimately failed, according to Wright, because it became the 'victim of the incompetence of its leaders and the incoherence of its programme' (1983: 159). Aside from 'preaching' abilities, Poujade himself apparently lacked all other organisational skills necessary to build and sustain a party.

The Progress parties were founded as *parties* that chose to participate in elections, but in the case of the Poujadist movement it was the other way around. The parliamentary group was organised after the election and there appears to have been no linkage between the original UDCA movement and the UFF party. According to Fiesci, the Poujadist movement's electoral success was due to what she calls 'rally politics'.[10] 'In France the rally drive and the party drive have been shaped by politicians' ambivalence toward representation and strong leadership within the republican framework sired by the Revolution' (Fieschi 2000: 74). The Poujadists mobilised voters protesting against the reforms and changes taking place in post–World War II France. This kind of mobilisation was difficult to adapt to parliamentary politics, according to Fieschi, as has often been the case with movements based on opposition to 'standard politics'. 'The UDCA was a *rally* and not a party. ... This should be understood as the all-encompassing reason for the UDCA's failure as a parliamentary group' (Fieschi 2000: 80). And according to Williams, 'negation and cynicism, xenophobia and violence were effective weapons for a lightning campaign but poor foundations for a lasting party' (1972: 168).

Seen against the backdrop of our multi-dimensional concept of institutionalisation, the Poujadists failed on all three dimensions. It appears to have had no organisational routines as a party, and the many defections among the MPs demonstrate lack of value infusion in the movement as such – as well as in Poujade. Moreover, it was not taken seriously by any other party, and it ultimately failed to develop durability. It was unable to survive the splits and defections in the parliamentary group. The reasons for the failure to institutionalise seem to be the inter-related problems of lack of strong and legitimate leadership, internal fractionalisation, and lack of a cohesive 'message'.

Sweden: New Democracy

In February 2000, the right-wing party New Democracy filed for bankruptcy, thus marking the formal end of a party that had burst on to the political arena in 1991.[11] The party won 6.7 per cent of the votes and twenty-five seats in the Swedish parliament, the Riksdag, in its debut election, but then lost all seats in the next election in 1994, polling only 1.2 per cent of the votes. In January 1995, opinion polls showed 0.5 per cent support, after which the party ceased to appear as a separate party in the polls.

The party may itself have contributed to its demise in three ways: internal rivalry, lack of party-building measures, and not being able to maintain itself as a party politically distinct from its rivals.

From the start, New Democracy had a potential for internal dissent in that it did not have *a* party leader, but rather was headed by a duo of political entrepreneurs: Ian Wachtmeister, a Swedish count and businessman; and Bert Karlsson, owner of an amusement park and a record studio. Wachtmeister quickly became the dominant figure of the two, but the duality symbolised an internal division within the party.

In 1994, after only three years' representation in the Riksdag, conflicts within New Democracy ripped the party apart. Wachtmeister was considered by his opponents to be 'undemocratic', managing the party as if it were a business concern. His supporters, on the other hand, saw the opponents as an undisciplined group bent on following populistic appeals rather than building a coherent policy alternative in Swedish politics. Increasingly, Wachtmeister and Karlsson also had different priorities, with Karlsson leaning closer to the Social Democrats on social welfare issues. In February 1995 Wachtmeister announced that he did not intend to run for re-election as head of the parliamentary group. His withdrawal unleashed a fierce internal struggle in which various factions claimed the right to the party leadership. At the party summit on 9–10 April, Harriett Colliander won the position. But her victory was disputed, which meant that an extra summit was summoned for 5 June. At this meeting, Vivianne Franzen was chosen as the party's leader. Colliander, in turn, refused to accept the result. A poll of all the party's members was carried out on 22 June, which resulted in support for Franzen of 80 per cent. The controversies continued throughout the summer, however, with lawsuits over who should represent the party. Thus, New Democracy went into the election campaign badly hurt from internal quarrelling and was abandoned by many of its original supporters.

A second problem was the party's organisation, or lack thereof. New Democracy's initial success depended heavily on the party's media attractiveness. It focused on issues neglected by the existing parties and its leaders adopted an unusual political style, similar to the founders of the Progress parties. In Sweden, it requires a considerable organisational mobilisation to be successful in local elections. But New Democracy emerged only half a year before the election as the initiative of the two founders, without any grass-root organisation to begin with. The lack of organisation on the ground was undoubtedly a factor in the party's differing amounts of success between the national and local levels in the 1991 elections, winning 6.7 per cent in the parliamentary election but just 3.4 per cent of the votes in the local elections.

In 1992 the party's first statutes were similar to those of most other Swedish parties, providing for a national organisation consisting of local chapters and individuals, but in reality the party was more like an exclusively national-level organisation. The lack of grass-root connections continued after the party had entered parliament. When the statutes were amended in 1993, they better reflected that reality, specifying now that the party would function only in national elections. Local branches were no longer described as the party's grass-root organisations, but instead as a form of 'cooperating party'. Local-level organisations ceased to have an automatic connection to the national level, but could enter into a 'contract' with the national party; such parties could not take part in local or provincial elections. An elaborate paragraph of the new statutes authorised a national-level 'statute committee' to deal with all conflicts of interpretations between New Democracy and 'the cooperating parties' (New Democracy, Statutes 1993), thus leaving the 'cooperating par-ties' with no influence in this process. When the party failed miserably at the national level in 1994, there was no organisational infrastructure to compen-sate for the lack of national leadership.

The 1992 rules also introduced a form of membership vote on candidate nominations that were to take place at the constituency level. But according to the amended rules of 1993, the party's executive committee had the right to appoint a nominating committee of five members whose task it was to nomi-nate the candidates. Thus, in two significant ways, New Democracy deviated radically from the organisation in existing parties. The explicit focus on national politics cut the party off from building a grass-roots organisational apparatus, and the central nominating committee introduced a procedure unknown to other parties. It is likely that these two measures scared away several prospective members and candidates, and probably hurt the party's image in public opinion as well.

Neither did it have any success in creating an identity that could tie voters to the party. At the time of its inception, party identification in Sweden had been in steady decline for three decades. Among New Democracy's voters in 1994, only 14 per cent expressed identification with the party, compared to older parties like the Social Democrats with 63 per cent and the Conser-vatives with 53 per cent (Gilljam and Holmberg 1995: 67).[12] The party won voters primarily from the Social Democratic Party (24 per cent), the Conser-vative Party (20 per cent), and from those who had not voted in the previous election (18 per cent) (Gilljam and Holmberg 1993: 231). At the same time, more than a third of New Democracy's voters claimed they favoured another party, most often the Moderates (Gilljam and Holmberg 1993: 242), indicat-ing a significant protest vote.

During the parliamentary term of 1991–94 the party also lost potential voters. In 1991, 7 per cent of respondents had New Democracy as their second choice among the parties, increasing to 9 per cent in 1993. But the rivalry within the party undercut that potential. In the 1994 elections, only

2 per cent of the electorate had New Democracy as a second choice (Oscarss-son 1998: 71).

Finally, a third form of self-inflicted harm was the party's own behaviour relative to other parties. Just as media access was important for New Democracy's initial success, media coverage during the 1991–94 parliament could have contributed to either improving or – as it happened – damaging the electorate's perception of the party. In the period between elections, the party's behaviour in parliament was important in this respect. The non-socialist minority government which was formed after the 1991 election had to rely on support from various parties in parliament. New Democracy usually supported the government in votes in the Riksdag (Mattson 1996). The alternative would have been to vote with the Social Democrats, which would in most cases have been even worse politically. However, by siding with the government on most votes, the party did not stand out as a separate and independent political alternative. A critical problem for parties is to become uniquely identified with a particular issue or set of issues in the electorate; New Democracy failed in this regard.

New Democracy was clearly an entrepreneurial party – though this time with *two* entrepreneurs at founding – which saw itself as anti-establishment. Although there were attempts to develop and routinise a normal party organisation, the choice of organisational model meant that there was hardly any opportunity for party members to influence decision-making in crucial areas, such as the nomination of office holders. The short time period during which the party existed was probably too brief for internal value infusion or external institutionalisation to have taken place.[13] The organisational model also proved incapable of dealing with party-building efforts on the ground, which would have been needed following the loss of all parliamentary seats in 1995. Lack of normal organisational routines and lack of acceptance of the official replacement for the party founder led to implosion and ultimate bankruptcy of the party.

There were many similar problems in the two Progress parties. However, when the construction of the party organisation started, the two Progress parties by and large followed a 'standard party model' that was common in Denmark and in Norway. This was in stark contrast to the experience of New Democracy. The problem was not that the leader(s) lacked organisational skills or ambition, but rather that they developed what proved to be a dysfunctional organisation.

Italy of Values (IdV)

Italy of Values (IdV) was established in 1998 by Antonio di Pietro. Di Pietro had already become famous as a prosecutor investigating corruption among senior politicians in the established parties. He had become a cabinet minister in the centre-left government from May to November 1996, resigning when he himself became a target of investigations for corruption. So, by the time di Pietro formed his new party, he had for a short period been part of the Italian 'system'. Thus the IdV's founder was something of a mixture of entrepreneur and insider, though his short time in political office justifies thinking of this as an entrepreneurial party.

According to Gianfranco Pasquino, IdV never established more than the minimum presence on the ground that was needed to nominate candidates: 'It was a group of politically ambitious individuals running for and holding office' (Pasquio 2014: 558). Although the party later (in 2010) attempted to improve its organisation, routinisation was never completed and the dominance of the party founder continued (Braghiroli et al. 2010: 92).

IdV was formed primarily in opposition to the Berlusconi government's 'waste of money'. It deviates from the right-wing Progress parties in being described as a centrist party, focused on moral issues, and throughout its history it was affiliated with alliances composed of left-leaning parties (Diamanti 2007). Di Pietro had joined the leftist coalition government in 1997, before forming the party. In the 2001 election the party ran on its own, winning one seat in the election that year, but the single MP who was elected defected to the Forza Italia (FI). In 2006 IdV took part in the left-wing coalition and participated in government. It won thirty-four seats of parliament, but lost one-fifth of them during the parliamentary term (Braghiroli et al. 2010). IdV's acceptance as a coalition and electoral alliance partner was probably not in recognition of the party becoming a likely long-term fixture on the political scene, but more a consequence of the electoral system in which a broad electoral alliance was necessary for any party to win in the election. Hence, it should not be interpreted as evidence of external institutionalisation in the eyes of the other parties.

The party did succeed to varying degrees in European and in local and regional elections, but in 2013 it lost its representation in parliament for the first time. The party participated in European elections in 2014, again without winning representation. After this, the party effectively disappeared.

Institutionalisation clearly did not proceed internally. Organisational improvements came late, and the party never overcame the dominance of the party founder. Internally in the parliamentary groups, there were several defections, indicating low internal value infusion.

IdV's failure to institutionalise seems to be linked to the party's weak presence on the ground and the continuous identification with the party founder, highlighted by the inclusion of di Pietro's name in the official logo of the party.

Netherlands: List Pim Fortuyn (LPF)

The Dutch party system has been significantly altered since the turn of the century[14] with several new parties winning office and some of them doing exceedingly well. One of these new parties, the List Pim Fortuyn, falls within the category of an entrepreneurial right-wing party, similar to the Progress parties.

The List Pim Fortuyn parallels the two Progress parties with regard to formation. The LPF was formed by a political outsider in February 2002, a few months before the election in which it was catapulted into parliament with twenty-six seats.

But there are also differences, even beyond the fact that the LPF's founder was assassinated one week before the List's first election.[15] While the Progress parties were shunned by the established parties in 1973, the LPF was immediately included in the coalition government that resulted from the 2002 election. But the party's experience in government and parliament was short lived. Three of its MPs defected from the party before the year was out and LPF withdrew from the government after just eighty-seven days, triggering a new election in early 2003. In that election the LPF lost eighteen of its twenty-six seats. During that parliamentary term, the remaining eight MPs defected to three other parliamentary parties and the party changed its parliamentary leader four times. All of its seats were lost in the following election in 2006 (Otjes 2011). Two years later the LPF was formally dissolved.

Thus, the LPF is an example of an entrepreneurial party which failed to institutionalise. De Lange and Art (de Lange and Art 2011) argue that the reason for its failure to institutionalise was linked to its sudden electoral success. That electoral success – and not least the inclusion in the government – meant that many completely new, inexperienced politicians obtained office. According to de Lange and Art, the elected representatives had a variety of motives for joining the party and strong party identity was not one of them. In the absence of the party founder and any successor with obvious leadership skills, the party's representatives were not able to act cohesively, and multiple conflicts ensued.[16] This stands in contrast to the dominance of Glistrup in Denmark and later Hagen in Norway.

Seen against the backdrop of our conceptual framework, the LPF did *not* institutionalise on any of the dimensions. The murder of the party founder shortly before the election in 2002 removed the party's leader before there were any procedures in place to deal with such a critical situation. Later attempts to build a routinised party organisation failed because of lack of commitments to the party as such (i.e. lack of internal value infusion) among the senior party actors, as indicated by the multiple defections among its MPs. Though the party immediately obtained external recognition by being included in the coalition government, this was due to the necessities of coalition formation rather than any assessment by other parties that LPF was likely to become a long-term force to be reckoned with. Though the party did, during its short span in parliament, affect the amount of attention given to immigration (Otjes 2011), it ultimately failed to gain objective durability as it chose to disband itself.

PARTIALLY INSTITUTIONALISED CASES

Italy: Five Star Movement (M5S)

The collapse of the Italian party system in the wake of the corruption scandals in the 1990s opened up opportunities for new parties. One of those party formations is the Five Star Movement, which was established in 2009. The initiative leading to the formation of the party was taken in 2005, when party founder Beppe Grillo started his blog and linked up with followers on online platforms (Mosca 2104).

M5S shares with the Progress parties its entrepreneurial character. The movement-turned-party was formed by the comedian Grillo and Gianberto Casaleggio, an IT-specialist. Grillo, like Anders Lange and Mogens Glistrup, did not intend initially to create a political party, but instead a movement (Bartlett et al. 2013).

M5S started as a movement opposed to the Italian political system, the political elite and the media (the press and television). A major criticism was that the elites had become disconnected from citizens; what was needed was a new form of communication between citizens and elected representatives. Thus, the similarity with the Progress parties is not only in the type of founders but also in the movements' criticism of 'the system'. Grillo shared with the founders of the Progress parties 'a distrust toward the state and all that is public' (Bordignon and Ceccarini 2015: 460). In this sense, M5S can be seen as a protest movement/protest party or an anti-party party.

But from the beginning the Progress parties were situated on the right, while M5S rejects the left-right dimension as being the central cleavage in Italian politics. According to Bordignon and Ceccarini 'it is positioned "beyond" ideologies' (2013: 427). The five-star symbol of the party refers to water, environment, mobility, development, and energy, which are not typically right-wing topics. The electoral programme of M5S is subdivided into seven points: state and citizens, energy, information, economy, transport, health, and education (Bordignon and Ceccarini 2015: 471); only the first of these is shared with the early Progress parties. The party has drawn supporters from across the political spectrum, first from the left, then from the right, and finally from the centre (Mosca 2104). A study of Grillo's Facebook followers (Bartlett et al. 2013) found a similar distribution across the left-right scale, but with the average location being slightly to the left of centre (3.88 on the scale from 1 (left) to 10 (right)).

While M5S started very much like anti-system movements/parties in organisational form, it nevertheless gradually changed to become more like traditional parties, though still with a very different type of organisational structure (Ceccarini and Bordignon 2016). Central to its organisation has been the combination of the internet and public events in city squares, with the internet serving as a mobilising instrument for the city meetings. In addition to blogs, Twitter and Facebook are used to link members with the leaders, somewhat similar to the approach of the Pirate parties. The M5S does not have regular party branches or a party headquarters but relies on 3000 Meet-up groups where its 300,000 members can participate. Members can present issues for discussion and vote for the nomination of candidates and for which issues should be in the party platform. Registered members cannot be members of other political parties and must agree with the principles of the MS5, similar to requirements in other parties.

However, in spite of the participatory character of the movement, in practice the two leaders have – to a great extent – been able to manage which issues should be discussed. The individual Meet-up groups function to allow local supporters to address a variety of local issues, but the *vertical* relationship between the groups and the leader(s) is characterised by top-down management (Bordignon and Ceccarini 2013: 438). Although members select the party's parliamentary candidates by voting online, it was only after pressure from the grass roots and the media that it was disclosed how many had participated in the process. And the votes for the individual nominees are not made public (Mosca 2104). The centralised nature of the organisation is illustrated by Article 3 of the seven articles regulating the organisation (Bordignon and Ceccarini 2013: 438). This article concerns the logo of the party, which is registered in the name of Beppe Grillo, who is the 'sole owner of the rights to use of the said logo' (438). The consequence of this rule is that Grillo himself can 'grant or refuse, maintain or withdraw, the political and electoral use of the symbol' (438). Thus, members, local groups, and representatives can be de facto expelled from the party/movement by the party founder. So Bordignon and Ceccarini concluded in 2015 that, in spite of the appearance of being somewhat institutionalised in the sense of de-personalisation and routinised procedures, the party was still very much a 'personal party' (2015: 465).

But in other ways, the party has indicated some tendency towards becoming more like other parties, organisationally speaking (Ceccarini and Bordignon 2016). As in the early phase of the Progress parties, Grillo's leadership position was not formalised through election, and the relationship between him and the parliamentary group was anything but routinised. MPs who pursued policies Grillo disagreed with were expelled from the party and critical comments to Grillo's blogs were removed (Mosca 2104). But there have been changes in the leadership approach. The original dual leadership has been supplemented by a 'five star *direttorio*', all five members of which are nominated by the two party leaders. According to Ceccarini and Bordignon (2016), this new unit indicates a process of normalisation of the party organisation. Grillo has taken a more backstage role and subsequently resumed his career as a comedian, while the other original founder, Casaleggio, passed away in the spring of 2016. Grillo has ceased to be the sole public face of the party as a younger member of the directorate, the twenty-nine-year-old vice-president of the Chamber of Deputies, has become the new public face. Following Ceccarini and Bordignon, these changes would appear to indicate that some level of routinisation has taken place.

Of the 163 members of the party elected in 2013, only 127 remained by August 2015, indicating lack of internal value infusion. Clearly, internal relationships between the party founder and the parliamentary group were still problematic. According to Natale:

> In the period immediately after the 2013 elections, the lack of an agreement with the PD for the formation of a government, as well as an attitude that could have appeared to reflect indifference to the future of Italy itself, led to some defections among those who had been elected under the M5S banner – especially among those who no longer identified with the leadership of Grillo and Casaleggio and disagreed with some of their statements. (2014: 32)

It is more difficult to assess the party's level of external institutionalisation from the vantage point of other parties, as its impact on governing has partly been 'negative' in refusing to enter into any alliance, either with the governing PD party or any of the opposition parties. Still, the party has clearly achieved a level of external recognition among the other parties. After winning some municipal seats in 2012, it had a dramatic national breakthrough in the parliamentary elections in 2013, winning 25.6 per cent of the votes and 163 seats. By refusing to enter into alliances, it forced the other parties to adopt a left-right governing coalition. With the party winning in June 2016 the mayoralty positions in Rome and Turin, two of the most significant municipal offices in the country, political competition in Italy has been altered. The party's refusal to negotiate with others has also been softened by discussions between the prime minister and Beppe Grillo on reform of the Italian electoral system, discussions which were transmitted online at the insistence of Grillo. And Bordignon and Ceccarini (2015: 465) argue that the party's success with getting many young and female MPs elected caused other parties to move in the same direction.

Ceccarini and Bordignon also find evidence of de-personalisation of the party in public opinion: 'In 2013, only 5% named a leader [of M5S] other than Grillo. This proportion grew to 34% in 2014, before reaching 48% in June 2015 and 6 7% in November of the same year" (147). Perhaps most importantly, the party's mayoral victories in 2016 occurred *after* the leadership transition.

At the time of writing, the party approaches its first decade of existence. It has developed and routinised several internal procedures and, most importantly, it has survived a transition of the leadership from its two original founders. Though institutionalisation is incomplete on some dimensions (e.g. external institutionalisation among the other parties and internal value infusion), evidence on other dimensions clearly indicates movement in the direction of institutionalisation. Ceccarinni and Bordignon (2016) are cautiously optimistic concerning the further *consolidation* of this party. With Grillo having effectively served as 'preacher' and then apparently easing a transition towards a more routinised, de-personalised type of organisation, it will now be up to the next generation of leadership to complete the organisation phase and to further establish what the party's role will be vis-à-vis other parties and government.

Italy: Forza Italia (FI)

Berlusconi's party, Forza Italia, was formed in 1993 and is archetypical of the 'personalistic party' (McDonnell 2013: 222). While the collapse of the Italian party system provided the fertile ground for new parties, it was Berlusconi's media assets that permitted him to construct a new party around himself, based on not only his personal financial assets but also the control of television networks (Fabbrini 2013). While positioned on the right in terms of economic policy, the FI differs from the Progress parties in that it was not – and is not today – a protest party.

The FI was created from above as an entrepreneurial party, but later developed structure resembling a more standard party organisation with local branches and members. Power, though, remained in the hands of the leader. In Donovan's words: 'Once Berlusconi was elected, the clubs[17] found they had no role in candidate selection or in shaping party policy. Hundreds collapsed' (Donovan 2015: 11).

So, in practice, the FI remained a personalistic, non-routinised, centralised party where, at the national level, officeholders' positions depended on their personal relationship with Berlusconi. The party 'on the ground' was deliberately designed to be weak (Paolucci 2006). McDonnell, writing in 2013, states: 'It is doubtful that the party on the ground ever became an autonomous force capable of surviving Berlusconi's departure, and the same seems to have been true of the PDL [which was the next iteration of the FI]'. Berlusconi's personal wealth meant that there was no need for the party to develop an organisation for the sake of mobilising resources. Indeed, the personalistic nature of the FI was highlighted in 2007 when Berlusconi unilaterally, without discussing with or informing anyone else, proclaimed that the FI in effect would be replaced by the PdL (Party of Liberty), through a merger with the AN (McDonnell 2013: 221). After McDonnell's article was published, Berlusconi once more 'changed' his party label and reverted to the FI, following the defection of parts of the old AN party in parliament. Through so many iterations – where Berlusconi himself was the most important symbol of continuity – it would seemingly have been difficult if not impossible to develop an overriding party culture and internal value infusion.[18]

In terms of external recognition, Berlusconi's parties are credited with having an impact, though not always in the way that was hoped for. Donovan (2015: 11), for example, argues that 'Silvio Berlusconi impacted massively on Italy's party politics. He restructured the right via Forza Italia and the People of Freedom co-creating a bipolar party system whilst championing a radical personalisation of politics. The new party system appeared to rotate around him, creating an unusual version of "moderate pluralism"'. Beyond "impact", the party clearly achieved external institutionalisation in the eyes of other parties, controlling the government for many years, including attracting coalition partners. Other parties had to conclude that the FI (or some version of the FI) would have to be taken into account, presumably for the long term.

At the time of writing, the FI party/ies together have persisted for more than two decades, during which they have displayed survivability, having lasted through three 'transformations' which included both mergers and splits.

But the key unanswered question concerning durability – and institutionalisation more generally – remains: what will happen if and when there is a transition to another leader? Berlusconi was an effective preacher for his new party, and was also effective in dealing with other parties in government, but development of de-personalised party organisation was neither his desire nor his forte. In the absence of routinised decision-making (in the hands of other than Berlusconi) and significant internal value infusion, the change of leadership will be the litmus test of further institutionalisation. McDonnell (2015) documents that even actors within the FI acknowledge the party's dependence on Berlusconi, and very few of them believe the PdL could have a future without him.[19] If that is the view of party insiders, it is reasonable to assume that others outside the party may share the same doubts.

An established record of durability does not guarantee permanence, and achievement of external institutionalisation does not assure that outsiders will continue to view the party in the same way in the absence of its central political figure. Donovan (2015: 11) has noted that the extreme personalisation of the party has already led to voter disillusionment and 'boosted support for a new party, the Five Star Movement. By 2014, it appeared that Berlusconi's major legacies were the rise of Matteo Renzi, the new prime minister and leader of the Democratic Party; his failure to construct an enduring, moderate conservative party; and the exceptional success of the Five Star Movement'. Without internal institutionalisation, an FI *without* Berlusconi could well be susceptible to de-institutionalisation on the other dimensions.

APPENDIX TABLE

Table A1 Comparative Cases of Personal Parties in Western Europe

		Entrepr[1]	Insider	Protest/ Anti-est[8]	Right-w[2]	Routinis[3]	Int val inf[4]	External-parties[9]	External-voters[10]	Surv[5]	Birthyr[6]	Status[7]
Poujadists (France)	UFF	y	–	y	y	n	n	n	n	n	1953	Failed; fizzled post 1958
New Democracy (Sweden)	ND	y	–	y	y	n	n	n	n	n	1991	Failed; bankrupt Feb 2000
Forza Italia (Italy)	FI	y	–	n	y (cr[11])	n	n	y	y[12]	y	1993	Partially; uncertain future
Italy of Values (Italy)	IdV	y	–	n	n (cl[13])	n	n	n	n	y	1998	Failed; fizzled after 2014 EU election
5-Star Movement (Italy)	M5S	y	–	y	n	y	?	?	y	y	2009	Partially institutionalised
List Pim Fortuyn (Ne)	LPF	y	–	y	y	n	n	n	n	n	2002	Disbanded itself in 2008
Party of Freedom (Ne)	PVV	–	y	y	y	n	n	?	?	?	2005/6	Unclear
Lega Ticino (Switz)	LT	y	–	y	y	n	n	y	y	y	1991	Partial; not internal
Progress (Norway)	FrP	y	–	y	y	y	y	y	y	y	1973	Institutionalised

	[1]	[2]	[3]	[4]	[5]			[8]	[9]	[10]	[6]	[7]
Progress (Denmark <95) FrP	y	y	y	–	y	y	y	opp	y	n	y	y	1972/3	Institutionalised
Progress (Denmark >95) FrP	y	y	y	–	y	y	y	opp	n	n	n	"	De-institutionalised

[1] Entrepreneurial party
[2] Right-wing
[3] Routinised procedures
[4] Internal value infusion
[5] Survivability
[6] Year of party birth
[7] To what extent is the party generally institutionalised?
[8] Anti-establishment
[9] Institutionalised in the eyes of other parties
[10] Institutionalised in the eyes of the electorate
[11] Centre-right
[12] The party did have a stable electoral core earlier; it is unclear now
[13] Centre-left

NOTES

1. While the UK Independence Party (UKIP) is often grouped together with the Progress parties as part of the same 'family of parties', UKIP itself is not a personal party in our conception of the term, even though its forerunner, the Anti-Federalist League (AFL) was an entrepreneurial party. AFL was established by the London School of Economics professor Alan Skid in 1991, in opposition to the Maastricht treaty. It failed in every election it took part in and faced competition also from the far better financed Referendum party, formed by a businessman in 1994, which also qualifies as an entrepreneurial party. These two parties were entrepreneurial, single issue parties, but they have in common a very short existence. The Referendum party disappeared when the party founder, James Goldsmith, died in 1997. The AFL was abandoned when Alan Skid, together with some of the Referendum party supporters established UKIP in 1994. After the 1997 election, in which all candidates except one had lost their deposits, Skid was 'forced' to resign from the party leadership and replaced by Nigel Farage, who would later become the dominating figure in the party. Therefore, UKIP's origin is clearly different from those of entrepreneurial parties.

2. The True Finns (now The Finns) is excluded here because it was not founded as a personal party. Instead it inherited an infrastructure from the recently bankrupt Finnish Rural Party (SMP). For more on the 'familial' relationship of the True Finns to two predecessor parties, see Arter (2012; 2016).

3. Lega Nord is excluded here primarily because we do not consider it to be a 'personal' party with a dominant founding leader. Also, the party was formed as a merger of existing regional leagues and some had already functioned as parties.

4. In a legal sense, it supposedly has two members: Geert Wilders himself and the 'Foundation Group Wilders', of which Geert Wilders is the only member, as a result of which Wilders is effectively the only member of the party. This odd legal construction allowed the party to register itself with the Electoral Committee (since under the Dutch electoral law, a political organisation can only be registered if it is an association and legal entity). The authors thank Ingrid van Biezen, University of Leiden, for information regarding the functioning of PVV.

5. According to de Lange and Art (2011), it is precisely the negative experience of another Dutch party, List Pim Fortuyn (LPF) (see below), that led Wilders to structure his party/movement in this way.

6. Twenty-seven national parties or groups nominated around 5000 candidates for the 1956 election.

7. But with the exceptions of the Communist and Socialist parties, all parties in the Fourth Republic suffered from indiscipline, so the Poujadists were not unique in this respect (Duncan MacRae 1967: 55ff).

8. That would also happen in the Danish Progress Party, but in that case it happened twenty years after its foundation.

9. The size of the parliamentary group, fifty-two MPs, may also have been more challenging to handle than the smaller groups of four and twenty-eight in, respectively, Norway and Denmark at the parties' electoral breakthroughs.

10. Rally politics refers to a style of politics 'heavily reliant on a rhetoric of unity and cohesion and will resort to mass gatherings most often around a prominent leader' while 'party politics privilege representational politics' (Fieschi 2000: 73).

11. The following is largely based on Svåsand and Wørlund (2001) and Svåsand and Wørlund (2005). See also Taggart (1996) for a comparative perspective on New Democracy and the Swedish Green Party.

12. However, although this may have contributed to its final demise, other new parties like the Green Party also scored low (19 per cent). Although the Greens lost all seats in 1991, they were able to make a comeback three years later.

13. Strøm (2016) states that all Swedish parties agreed not to have any political linkages with New Democracy when the party emerged during the 1991 election campaign, but in a study of party policy positions in the Swedish parliament (Riksdagen) she found that both the Social Democrats and the Conservative Party (Moderaterna) moved *slightly* towards the position of New Democracy during the parliamentary term 1991–95. This was mainly because the parties realised that immigration would become a more important issue in future elections. Before the next election New Democracy had made itself irrelevant due to the internal conflicts.

14. See Dorussen 2004: 132.

15. Pim Fortuyn was a professor of sociology, and, although an active debater on political issues, he did not hold any offices until he was elected chairperson of the new Livable Netherlands party in November 2001. He was removed from that office after a few months and immediately founded the LPF.

16. 'Moreover, as a consequence of the continuous in-fighting, the turnover in party leaders and chairs was extremely high and the number of party splits significant' (de Lange and Art, 2011: 1237).

17. The basic party units of the FI.

18. Partial evidence of this came in 2011, when at least half a dozen members of the parliamentary group defected over the Berlusconi government's handling of the Euro crisis. For context, see *The Guardian,* https://www.theguardian.com/world/2011/nov/03/silvio-berlusconi-resignation-euro-crisis, accessed on 13 January 2017.

19. It is noteworthy that the party's dependence on Berlusconi is not only for leadership, but also for finances. Hopkin (2004: 634) says that 'Berlusconi employed substantial financial and human resources of companies under his control in the formation of the party'.

References

Allern, E. H., and K. Heidar. 2001. 'Partier og interesseorganisasjoner i Norge.' In *Partier och Interesseorganisationer i Norden*, edited by Jan Sundberg, 103–40. Copenhagen: Nordisk Ministerråd.

Allern, E. H., K. Heidar and R. Karlsen. 2016. *After the Mass Party: Continuity and Change in Political Parties and Representation in Norway*. London: Lexington Books.

Akkerman, T. 2016. 'The Party for Freedom: Balancing between mission, votes and office.' In *Radical Right-Wing Populist Parties in Western Europe,* edited by T. Akkerman, S. L. de Lange and M. Rooduijn, 144–68. London: Routledge.

Andersen, J., and T. Bjørklund. 1990. 'Structural changes and new cleavages: The Progress Parties in Denmark and Norway.' *Acta Sociologica* 33 (3): 195–217.

Arter, D. 1999. 'Party system change in Scandinavia since 1970: "Restricted change" or "general change".' *West European Politics* 22 (3): 139–58.

Arter, D. 2012. 'Analysing "successor parties": The case of the True Finns.' *West European Politics* 35 (4): 803–25.

Arter, D. 2016. 'When new party X has the "X factor": On resilient entrepreneurial parties.' *Party Politics* 22 (1): 15–26.

Arter, D., and E. Kestilä-Kekkonen. 2014. 'Measuring the extent of party institutionalisation: The case of a populist entrepreneur party.' *West European Politics* 37 (5): 932–56.

Bartlett, J., C. Froio, M. Litter and D. McDonnell. 2013. *'Social Media is Changing Politics Across Europe ...' New Political Actors in Europe: Beppe Grillo and the M5S*. London: Demos.

Basedau, M., and A. Stroh. 2008. 'Measuring party institutionalization in developing countries: A new research instrument applied to 28 African political parties.' *GIGA Working Paper* 69: 1–28.

Berglund, S., and U. Lindstrøm. 1978. *The Scandinavian Party System(s)*. Lund: Studentlitteratur.

Bergman, T., and K. Strøm, eds. 2010. *The Madisonian Turn: Political Parties and Parliamentary Democracy in Nordic Europe*. Ann Arbor, MI: University of Michigan Press.

Bille, L. 1991. 'The Danish Party Organizations and the Thesis of Party Decline.' Presented at the XVth World Congress of the International Political Science Association, Buenos Aires.

Bille, L. 1992. 'Denmark.' In *Party Organizations: A Data Handbook on Party Organizations in Western Democracies, 1960–90*, edited by R. S. Katz and P. Mair, 199–272. London: Sage.

Bille, L. 1994. 'Denmark: The decline of the membership party.' In *How Parties Organize: Change and Adaptation in Party Organizations in Western Democracies*, edited by R. S. Katz and P. Mair, 143–57. London: Sage.

Bille, L. 1998. *Dansk Partipolitik 1987–1998*. Copenhagen: Jurist-og Økonomforbundets Forlag.

Bille, L. 1997. *Partier i Forandring*. Odense: Odense Universitetsforlag.

Bille, L., and F. J. Christiansen. 2001. 'Partier og interesseorganisationer i Danmark.' In *Partier och Interesseorganisationer i Norden*, edited by Jan Sundberg, 29–78. Copenhagen: Nordisk Ministerråd.

Bolleyer, N. 2013. *New Parties in Old Party Systems. Persistence and Decline in Seventeen Democracies*. Oxford: Oxford University Press.

Bordignon, F., and L. Ceccarini. 2013. 'Five Stars and a Cricket. Bepe Grillo shakes Italian politics.' *South European Society and Politics* 18 (4): 427–49.

Bordignon, F., and L. Ceccarini. 2015. 'The five-star movement: a hybrid actor in the net of state institutions.' *Journal of Modern Italian Studies* 20 (4): 454–73.

Borre, O. 1992. 'Denmark.' In *Electoral Change. Respons to Evolving Social and Attitudinal Structures in Western Countries*, edited by T. T. Mackie, M. N. Franklin, H. Valen et al., 153–72. Cambridge: Cambridge University Press.

Braghiroli, S., L. Verzichelli, and D. Bull. 2010. 'Condemned to ineffectiveness? The PD and IdV between opposition and coalition strategies much ado about nothing?' *Italian Politics* 26: 85–102.

Burns, J. M. 1978. *Leadership*. New York: Harper Torchbooks.

Castles, F. 1986. 'Social expenditure and the Political Right: a methodological note.' *European Journal of Political Research* 14 (5–6): 669–76.

Ceccarini, L., and F. Bordignon. 2016. 'The five stars continue to shine: the consolidation of Grillo's "movement party" in Italy.' *Contemporary Italian Politics* 8 (2): 131–59.

Christensen, D. A. 1994. 'Fornyinga av Bondepartia i Sverige og Noreg.' In *Partiene i en brytningstid*, 327–55. Bergen: Alma Mater.

Damborg, P., and T. Østerby. 1973. *Glistrups Lille sorte*. Copenhagen: Chr. Erichsens Forlag.

Damgaard, E. 2010. 'Change and Challenges of Danish Parliamentary Democracy.' In *The Madisonian Turn: Political parties and parliamentary democracy in Nordic Europe*, edited by T. Bergman and K. Strøm, 67–111. Ann Arbor, MI: University of Michigan Press.

DeClair, E. G. 1999. *Politics on the Fringe: The People, Policies, and Organization of the French Front National.* Durham, NC: Duke University Press.

de Lange, S. L., and D. Art. 2011. 'Fortuyn versus Wilders: An agency-based approach to radical right party building.' *West European Politics* 34 (6): 1229–49.

Diamanti, I. 2007. 'The Italian centre-right and centre-left: Between parties and "the party".' *West European Politics* 30 (4): 733–62.

Donovan, M. 2015. 'Berlusconi's impact and legacy: Political parties and the party system.' *Modern Italy* 20 (1): 11–24.

Dorussen, H. 2004. 'Pim Fortuyn and the "new" far right in the Netherlands.' *Representation* 40 (2): 131–45.

Einhorn, E. S., and J. Logue. 1988. 'Continuity and Change in the Scandinavian Party Systems.' In *Parties and Party Systems in Liberal Democracies*, edited by S. B. Wolinetz, 159–202. New York: Routledge.

Einhorn, E. S., and J. Logue. 1989. *Modern Welfare States: Politics and Policies in Social Democratic Scandinavia.* New York: Praeger.

Fabbrini, S. 2013. 'The rise and fall of Silvio Berlusconi: Personalization of politics and its limits.' *Comparative European Politics* 11 (2): 153–71.

Fieschi, C. 2000. 'Rally politics and political organisation: An institutionalist perspective on the French far right.' *Modern & Contemporary France* 8 (1): 71–89.

Fitzgerald, S. 1970. 'The anti-modern rhetoric of Le Mouvement Poujade.' *The Review of Politics* 32 (2): 167–90.

Folketinget. 1973. *Folketingets Håndbog.* Copenhagen: Folketinget.

Formisano, R. P. 1974. 'Deferential-participant politics. The early republic's political culture; 1790–1840.' *American Political Science Review* 68 (2): 473–87.

Frankland, E. G. 1995. 'Germany: The rise, fall and recovery of Die Grünen.' In *The Green Challenge: The Development of Green Parties in Europe*, edited by D. Richardson and C. Rootes, 17–33. New York: Routledge.

Fremskridtspartiet. 1996. *Fremskridtspartiets Historie, 1973–1996.* Copenhagen.

Gilljam, M., and S. Holmberg. 1993. *Valjarna Inför 90-talet.* Stockholm: Fritzes.

Gilljam, M., and S. Holmberg. 1995. *Valjarnas Val.* Stockholm: Fritzes.

Glasser, R. 1994. *Høyre og gaullistene: sommerfuglene under lampeskjermen?: konservative partiers reaksjoner på nye radikale høyre partier i Norge og Frankrike.* Unpublished Master's thesis. University of Bergen.

Glistrup, M. 1978. 'Information Document on the Danish Progress Party.' Presented at the European Parliament, Brussels. Unpublished.

Green, J. C., and W. Binning. 1997. 'Surviving Perot: The origins and future of the Reform Party.' In *Multiparty Politics in America,* edited by P. S. Herrnson and J. C. Green, 87–102. Lanham, MD: Rowman and Littlefield Publishers.

Gudbrandsen, F. 2010. 'Partisan influence on immigration: The case of Norway.' *Scandinavian Political Studies* 33 (3): 248–70.

Gurr, T. R. 1974. 'Persistence and change in political systems, 1800–1971.' *American Political Science Review* 68 (4): 1482–504.

Hagen, C. I. 1984. *Ærlighet Varer Lengst.* Oslo: Aventura.

Hagen, C. I. 2007. *Ærlig Talt: Memoarer 1944–2007.* Oslo: J. W. Cappelen.

Hahn-Pedersen, M. 1981. *Historien om et Nul: Mogens Glistrup og Fremskridtsbevægelsen 1971–73.* Odense: Odense universitetsforlag.

Harmel, R., and R. K. Gibson. 1995. 'Right-libertarian parties and the "new values": A re-examination.' *Scandinavian Political Studies* 18 (2): 97–118.

Harmel, R., and K. Janda. 1982. *Parties and Their Environments. Limits to Reform?* London: Longman.

Harmel, R., and J. D. Robertson. 1985. 'Formation and success of new parties: A cross-national analysis.' *International Political Science Review* 6 (4): 501–24.

Harmel, R., and K. Janda. 1994. 'An integrated theory of party goals and party change.' *Journal of Theoretical Politics* 6 (3): 259–87.

Harmel, R., and L. Svåsand. 1989. 'From Protest to Party: Progress on the Right in Denmark and Norway.' Presented at the Annual Meeting of the American Political Science Association, Atlanta.

Harmel, R., and L. Svåsand. 1993. 'Party Leadership and Party Institutionalization.' *West European Politics* 16 (2): 67–88.

Harmel, R., and L. Svåsand. 1997. 'The influence of new parties on old parties' platforms: The Cases of the Progress Parties and Conservative Parties of Denmark and Norway.' *Party Politics* 3 (3): 315–40.

Harmel, R., and A. Tan. 1996. Dominant factions. Party change project data, Texas A&M University. Unpublished; available from Robert Harmel at Texas A&M University or online at https://pols.tamu.edu/wp-content/uploads/sites/16/2015/09/PCP_domfacanc.pdf.

Heidar, K., and L. Svåsand, eds. 1994. *Partiene i en Brytningstid.* Bergen: Alma Mater.

Heidar, K., and L. Svåsand, eds. 1997. *Partier Uten Grenser?* Oslo: TANO-Aschehoug.

Helmke, G., and S. Levitsky. 2004. 'Informal institutions and comparative politics: A research agenda.' *Perspectives on Politics* 2 (4): 725–40.

Hermann, M. G. 1986. 'Ingredients of Leadership.' *Political Psychology. Contemporary Problems and Issues,* 167–92.

Hirsch, J., 1998. 'A party is not a movement and vice versa.' In *The German Greens: Paradox Between Movement and Party,* edited by M. Mayer and J. Ely, 180–209. Philadelphia: Temple University Press.

Hopkin, J. 2004. 'The problem with party finance: Theoretical perspectives on the funding of party politics.' *Party Politics* 10 (6): 627–51.

Huntington, S. 1965. 'Political development and political decay.' *World Politics* 17 (3): 386–430.

Huntington, S. 1968. *Political Order in Changing Societies.* New Haven, CT: Yale University Press.

Ivarsflaten, E., and F. Gudbrandsen. 2012. 'The populist radical right in Western Europe.' In *Europa Regional Surveys of the World: Western Europe 2012 (16th ed.)*, edited by J. Lov, 1–5. London: Routledge.

Iversen, J. M. 1998. *Fra Anders Lange til Carl I. Hagen: 25 år med Fremskrittspartiet*. Oslo: Millenium.

Janda, K. 1980. *Political Parties: A Cross-National Survey*. New York: Free Press.

Janda, K., and R. Gillies. 1980. 'Continuity and Change.' *Political Parties: A Cross-National Survey*, 162–69. New York: Free Press.

Jupskås, A. R. 2015. *The Persistence of Populism. The Norwegian Progress Party 1973–2009*. Unpublished PhD dissertation, University of Oslo.

Katz, D. 1973. 'Patterns of leadership.' In *Handbook of Political Psychology*, edited by J. N. Knutson, 203–33. San Francisco: Jossey Bass Publishers.

Kjærsgaard, P. 1998. *- men udsigten er god …* Copenhagen: Peter Asschenfeldts nye Forlag.

Kosiara-Pedersen, K. 2015. 'Party membership in Denmark: Fluctuating membership figures and organizational stability.' *Party Members and Activists*, edited by In E. van Haute and A. Gauja, 66–83. Routledge: London.

Kostadinova, T., and B. Levitt. 2014. 'Toward a theory of personalist parties: Concept formation and theory building.' *Politics & Policy* 42 (4): 490–512.

Kuhnle, S. 1983. *Velferdsstatens Utvikling: Norge i komparativt perspektiv*. Oslo: Universitetsforlaget.

Larsen, B. V. 1978. 'En studie af Fremskridtspartiets organisation.' *Politica* 3 (4): 59–84.

Levitsky, S. 1998. 'Institutionalization and Peronism: the concept , the case and the case for unpacking the concept.' *Party Politics* 4 (1): 77–92.

Levitt, B., and T. Kostadinova. 2014. 'Personalist Parties in the Third Wave of Democratization: A Comparative Analysis of Peru and Bulgaria.' *Politics & Policy* 42 (4): 513–47.

Lindstrøm, U. 1985. *Fascism in Scandinavia 1920–1940*. Stockholm: Almqvist & Wicksell.

Lipset, S. M., and S. Rokkan. 1967. 'Cleavage structures, party systems and voter alignments: An introduction.' In *Party Systems and Voter Alignments*, edited by S. M. Lipset and S. Rokkan, 1–64. New York: Free Press.

Lowery, D., A. van Witteloostuijn, G. Péli, H. Brasher, S. Otjes, and S. Gherghina. 2013. 'Policy agendas and births and deaths of political parties.' *Party Politics* 19 (3): 381–407.

Lupu, Noam. 2009. 'Nationalization and party institutionalization in twentieth-century Argentina.' Unpublished paper available at http://www.noamlupu.com/nationalization.pdf

MacRae, Jr., D. 1967. *Parliament, Parties and Society in France 1946–1958*. New York: St. Martin's Press.

Marcum, J. A. 1959. 'French party literature.' *Western Political Quarterly* 12 (1): 168–76.

Mattson, I. 1996. 'Negotiations in parliamentary committees.' In *The Bargaining Democracy*, edited by L.G. Stenelo and M. Jerneck, 61–144. Lund: Lund University Press.

Mazzoleni, O., and G. Voerman. 2017. 'Memberless parties: Beyond the business-firm party model?' *Party Politics* 23 (6): 783–92.

McDonnell, D. 2013. 'Silvio Berlusconi's personal parties: From Forza Italia to the Popolo Della Libertà.' *Political Studies* 61 (1): 217–33.

McDonnell, D. 2016. 'Populist leaders and coterie charisma.' *Political Studies* 64 (3): 719–33.

McHale, V. E., ed. 1983. *Political Parties of Europe*. Westport CT: Greenwood Press.

Meguid, B. M. 2001. 'Competing with the neophyte: The role of mainstream party strategy in rising party success.' Presented at the Annual Meeting of the American Political Science Association, San Francisco.

Mosca, L. 2014. 'The Five Star Movement: Exception or Vanguard in Europe?' *The International Spectator* 49 (1): 36–52.

Mueller, S., and O. Mazzoleni. 2016. 'Regionalist protest through shared rule? Peripherality and the use of cantonal initiatives in Switzerland.' *Regional & Federal Studies* (26) 1: 45–71.

Narud, H. M., and K. Strøm. 2010. 'Norway: From Hønsvaldian parliamentarism back to Madisonian roots.' In *The Madisonian Turn: Political parties and parliamentary democracy in Nordic Europe*, edited by T. Bergman and K. Strøm, 200–50. Ann Arbor, MI: University of Michigan Press.

Natale, P. 2014. 'The birth, early history and explosive growth of the Five Star Movement.' *Contemporary Italian Politics* 6 (1): 16–36.

Neustadt, R. E. 1960. *Presidential Power: The Politics of Leadership*. New York: Wiley.

Offe, C. 1988. 'From youth to maturity: the challenge of party politics.' In *The German Greens: Paradox Between Party and Movement*, edited by M. M. and J. Ely, 165–79. Philadelphia: Temple University Press.

Oliver, C. 1992. 'The Antecedents of deinstitutionalization.' *Organization Studies* 13 (4): 563–88.

Otjes, S. 2011. 'The Fortuyn effect revisited: How did the LPF affect the Dutch parliamentary party system?' *Acta Politica* 46 (4): 400–24.

Panebianco, A. 1988. *Political Parties: Organization and Power*. New York: Cambridge University Press.

Paolucci, C. 2006. 'The nature of Forza Italia and the Italian transition.' *Journal of Southern Europe and the Balkans Online* 8 (2): 163–78.

Pasquino, G. 2014. 'Italy: The triumph of Personalist Parties.' *Politics & Policy* 42 (4): 548–66.

Pedahzur, A., and A. Brichta. 2002. 'The institutionalization of extreme right-wing charismatic parties: A paradox?' *Party Politics* 8 (1): 31–49.

Pedersen, K. 1997. *Fremskridtspartiet - De første 25 år i dansk politik*. Skjærbæk: Fremskridtspartiets forlag.

Pedersen, M. N. 1987. 'The Danish "working multiparty system": Breakdown or adaptation?' In *Party Systems in Denmark, Austria, the Netherlands and Belgium*, edited by H. Daalder, 1–60. London: Francis Pinter.

Pedersen, M. N. 1988. 'The defeat of all parties: The Danish Folketing election 1973.' In *When Parties Fail. Emerging Alternative Organizations*, edited by K. Lawson and P. H. Merkl, 257–81. Princeton: Princeton University Press.

Petersen, N., and P. Svensson. 1989. 'Valgenes politiske sammenhæng.' In *To Folketingsvalg. Vælgerholdninger og vælgeradfærd i 1987 og 1988*, edited by J. Elklit and O. Tonsgaard, 22–51. Århus: Forlaget Politica.

Poguntke, T. 1996. 'Anti-party sentiment – Conceptual thoughts and empirical evidence: Explorations into a minefield.' *European Journal of Political Research* 29 (3): 319–44.

Poguntke, T., and S. E. Scarrow. 1996. 'The politics of anti-party sentiment: Introduction.' *European Journal of Political Research* 29 (3): 257–62.

Polsby, N. W. 1968. 'The Institutionalization of the U. S. House of Representatives.' *American Political Science Review* 68 (1): 144–68.

Punnett, R. M. 1992. *Selecting the Party Leader. Britain in Comparative Perspective*. London: Harvester-Wheatsheaf.

Randall, V., and L. Svåsand. 2002. 'Party Institutionalization in New Democracies.' *Party Politics* 8 (1): 5–29.

Rose, R., and T. T. Mackie. 1988. 'Do Parties Persist or Fail? The Big Trade-Off Facing Organizations.' In *When Parties Fail: Emerging Alternative Organizations*, edited by K. Lawson and P. H. Merkl, 533–58. Princeton: Princeton University Press.

Sankiaho, R. 1971. 'A Model of the Rise of Populism and Support for the Finnish Rural Party.' *Scandinavian Political Studies* 6 (6): 27–47.

Sartori, G. 1976. *Parties and Party Systems*. Cambridge: Cambridge University Press.

Sauerberg, S. 1988. 'The general election in Denmark 1988.' *Scandinavian Political Studies* 11 (4): 361–71.

Schedler, A. 1996. 'Anti-political establishment parties.' *Party Politics* 2 (3): 291–312.

Selznick, P. 1957. *Leadership in Administration: A Sociological Interpretation*. New York: Harper & Row.

Shields, J. G. 2004. 'An enigma still: Poujadism fifty years on.' *French Politics, Culture & Society* 22 (1): 36–56.

Skjeie, H. 1999. *Vanens Makt. Styringstradisjoner i Arbeiderpartiet*. Oslo: Ad Notam Gyldendal.

Stein, M. B. 1973. *The Dynamics of Right-Wing Protest: A Political Analysis of Social Credit in Quebec*. Toronto: University of Toronto Press.

Stinchcombe, A. L. 1965. 'Social structure and organizations.' In *Handbook of Organizations*, edited by J. G. March, 142–93. Chicago: Rand McNall.

Strøm, A. 2016. 'Nya utmanare – nya strategier? Etablerade partier bemöter ny konkurrens.' Examensarbete, Kandidatuppsats, Högskolan i Dalarna. Available at: http://www.diva-portal.org/smash/record.jsf?pid=diva2%3A943729&dswid=-3565. Accessed 30 May 2017.

Strøm, K. 1986. 'Deferred gratification and minority governments in Scandinavia.' *Legislative Studies Quarterly* 11 (4): 583–605.

Strøm, K., and J. Y. Leipart. 1989. 'Ideology, strategy and party competition in postwar Norway.' *European Journal of Political Research* 17 (3): 263–88.

Svåsand, L. 1992. 'Norway.' In *Party Organizations: A Data Handbook on Party Organizations in Western Democracies, 1960–90*, edited by R. S. Katz and P. Mair, 732–80. London: Sage.

Svåsand, L., and I. Wørlund. 2005. 'Partifremvekst og partioverlevelse: Fremskrittspartiet og Ny Demokrati.' In *Partiernas Århundrade : fempartimodellens uppgång och fall i Norge och Sverige,* edited by M. Demker and L. Svåsand, 253–79. Stockholm: Santerus.

Taggart, P. A. 1996. *The New Populism and the New Politics. New Protest Parties in Sweden in Comparative Perspective*. Houndmills: Macmillan.

Togeby, L. 1992. 'The nature of declining party membership in Denmark: Causes and consequences.' *Scandinavian Political Studies* 15 (1): 1–19.

Valen, H. 1981. *Valg og Politik*. Oslo: NKS-forlaget.

Veugelers, J. W. P. 1995. *The Institutionalization of France's Front National*. Unpublished thesis, Princeton University.

Vossen, K. 2010. 'Populism in the Netherlands after Fortuyn: Rita Verdonk and Geert Wilders compared.' *Perspectives on European Politics and Society* 11 (1): 22–38.

Webster's New World College Dictionary. 2010. Fourth edition, Cleveland: Wiley Publishing, Inc.

Wellhofer, E. S. 1972. 'Stratification, rationality, and behavior: Tests with political party elites.' Unpublished paper, Michigan State University.

Whetten, D. A. 1980. 'Sources, Responses, and Effects of Organizational Decline.' In *The Organizational Life Cycle*, edited by J. R. Kimberly, R. H. Miles and Associates. San Francisco: Jossey-Bass.

Widtfeldt, A. 2000. 'Scandinavia: Mixed success for the populist right.' *Parliamentary Affairs* 43 (3): 486–500.

Williams, P. M. 1970. *French Politicians & Elections 1951–1969*. Cambridge: Cambridge University Press.

Williams, P. M. 1972. *Crisis of Compromise: Politics in the Fourth Republic*. London: Longman.

Worre, T. 1980. 'Class parties and class voting in the Scandinavian countries.' *Scandinavian Political Studies* 3 (4): 299–320.

Wright, V. 1983. *The Government and Politics of France*. London: Hutchinson.

Wörlund, I., and L. Svåsand. 2001. 'The rise and fall of the Swedish party New Democracy.' Presented at the Annual Meeting of the American Political Science Association, San Fransisco.

INTERNET SOURCES

https://www.theguardian.com/world/2011/nov/03/silvio-berlusconi-resignation-euro-crisis. Accessed 13 January 2017.

http://www.parties-and-elections.eu/denmark2a.html. Accessed 14 January 2017.

http://www.parties-and-elections.eu/norway2.html. Accessed 14 January 2017.

http://www.ft.dk/folketinget/oplysningen/regeringer/regeringer_siden_1953.aspx. Accessed 14 January 2017.

http://nkp.no. Accessed 8 March 2017.

http://www.regjeringen.no/nn/om-regjeringa/tidligere/oversikt/ministerier_regjeringer/nyere_tid/regjeringer.html?id=438715. Accessed 14 January 2017.

http://www.statistikbanken.dk/statbank5a/default.asp?w=1745. Accessed 14 January 2017.

Merriam-Webster (www.merriam-webster.com).

The Free Dictionary (www.thefreedictionary.com).

Index

About the Contributors

Robert Harmel (1950) Professor, Department of Political Science, Texas A&M University, College Station, Texas, USA.

Lars G. Svåsand (1947) Professor, Department of Comparative Politics, University of Bergen, Norway.

Hilmar Mjelde (1981) Post doc, Department of Information Science and Media Studies, University of Bergen, Norway; Senior Researcher, The Uni Research Rokkan Center, Norway.

www.ingramcontent.com/pod-product-compliance
Lightning Source LLC
Chambersburg PA
CBHW021818270326
41932CB00007B/234